MY LIFE *as a*
GAY MAN
in a STRAIGHT
WOMAN'S BODY

MY LIFE *as a*

GAY MAN

in a STRAIGHT

WOMAN'S BODY

AN AUTOBIOGRAPHY

by
Carol Sherman-Jones

Five Star Publications, Inc.
P.O. Box 6698
Chandler, AZ 85246-6698

Library of Congress Cataloging-in-Publication Data

Sherman-Jones, Carol, 1961–
    My life as a gay man in a straight woman's body: an autobiography / by Carol Sherman-Jones
    p. cm.
  ISBN: 1-58985-004-1 (perfect bound)
    1. Sherman-Jones, Carol, 1961– 2. Women—Ohio—Cincinnati—Biography.
    3. Businesswomen—Ohio—Cincinnati—Biography. 4. Gay men—Relations with heterosexual women—Ohio—Cincinnati. 5. Women-owned business enterprises—Ohio—Cincinnati. 6. Gay Bars—Ohio—Cincinnati. I. Title.

HQ1413.S45 A3 2001
305.h'092—dc21=
[B]   20011033829
        Printed in the United States of America
FIRST EDITION

PUBLISHED BY
Five Star Publications, Inc.

PUBLISHING CONSULTANT
Linda F. Radke

SENIOR EDITORIAL CONSULTANT
Paul M. Howey

EDITOR
Sue Ellen Brown

BOOK DESIGN
Barbara Kordesh

PROOFREADER
Sue DeFabis

COVER PHOTO
by Joseph Fuqua II
with permission from the *Cincinnati Enquirer*

DEDICATION

To Elinor Sherman, my mother whose voice
continues to strengthen my soul.
I would have never made it so fine if I hadn't heard it.
You've taught me so much and I will pass it on.

To my sister Nancy Sherman-White
who reminds me that no matter how far apart we are,
we are looking at the same moon.

To my husband Don for wanting me to be whatever
I want to be and for giving me big love to achieve it.

To my stepdaughter Amy Marie Jones for allowing me to reap
the joys of motherhood without having to give birth.

To my friend and editor Sue Ellen Brown for
spotting a diamond in a mound of garbage—
there can never be enough chocolate chip cookies!

To Steve, Rob, Paula, David, and Greg
for accepting me "as is" and loving me
anyway…I'm sure we've been around before.

And to my father, for you and I
have proved that it's never too late.

CONTENTS

THE AUDITION

THE REHEARSAL

Contents

THE SHOW—ACT I

INTERMISSION

THE SHOW—ACT II

Contents

ENCORE!

My Life as a Gay Man in a Straight Woman's Body
is much more than the entertaining "slice of life" story
of Carol Sherman-Jones.

Carol, one of Cincinnati's most energetic and in-your-
face personalities is also one of our finest non-gay allies.
She takes the reader through her life which has been, at
least thus far, both troubled and triumphant. She offers
an honest assessment of both her gifts and difficult life
struggles. Carol invites the reader into interesting
vignettes of her history…well written and presented in
her own colorful descriptions and charming but blunt
style. While her writing style is entertaining, the reader
will come away feeling privileged to have been included
on the painful road of a woman whose life journey
toward recovery has a message of hope and joyful
inclusion for all—gay, straight, or…well…whatever.

Cincinnatians who frequented either or both of
Carol's wonderful restaurants will sit back to remember
how it felt to be a part of Carol's social family.
Romances started and ended there. Friendships were
developed and our communities learned the news of one
another while intersecting with fellow travelers and
partyers. Carol learned to make a place for herself in
the world and then opened the door for the rest of us
to join the celebration. Thanks, Carol!

—CHERYL EAGLESON
CO-PRODUCER OF *ALTERNATING CURRENTS*,
CINCINNATI'S GLBT PUBLIC AFFAIRS RADIO PROGRAM

GRATEFUL
ACKNOWLEDGMENTS

I wish to recognize some people from Rusconi's who gave me the love to love myself: Chuck Schuler, Vermont Reynolds, Darrel Combs, Patrick Korb, Al Rienart, Turkey, Andrea Lippelman, Mr. Bushken, Ge-Ann Hays, Tom Conway, Tim Benton, John Hohensinner, Bruce Strong, Ray Roberts, Jason Schmidt, Patrick McNamara, Rob Goldberg, Matt Rost, Susan Peskin, Mark Draves, Doug Baldridge, Larry Moore, David Tape, Randy Bishop, Don Creasey, Ivan Daniels, BB, Chiquita, Bill Phelan, Jim Canter, John Harrison, Bob Range, Josie Thiesman, Eric Lafferty, Don Reese, Shirley Jester, Rick Spare…and there are so many more of you who helped save my life. How can I thank you? (Don't even think of asking for royalties from this book though!)

Thanks also to Susan Corken, who took the time to read the rough draft and for adding an extra blaze of fire inside of me, by *knowing* that this book would be a smash hit. Hugs to Nancy Blignaut my English teacher at Northern Kentucky University, who told me I was a writer before I knew I was. Coodles to Hector Polanco, whose counsel consoled me. Kisses to the Chatinskys' and the Estrins' for not only being my parents' friends, but mine, too.

Bows to Linda Radke, of Five Star Publications, for her patience, belief and love. And for going over and above the call of duties to make this book a success. I'm glad she listens to the messages given to her by the Universe. What can I say to Paul Howey, Senior Editorial Consultant? For all of his humor and tireless effort in wanting this manuscript to be the best it can possibly be—bris or not, he and I are definitely related. He's tops in my book.

I know proper etiquette in the "book world" is to either name a person in the dedication *or* the acknowledgment page. However, Sue Ellen Brown, proprietor of Justified Left—A Publishing Alliance, deserves both. The work she did is beyond words. Her endless trips to my house where she prodded my brain with her spirited belief and tuned knowledge (while spiraling on caffeine and chocolate) kept this project tight and visible. I can honestly say I could never have done it without her expertise and pats on my back.

I can't express enough love to Mary Pierce-Brosmer who founded "Women Writing for (a) Change," a school in Cincinnati for women writers. Without her support and the embrace of my sister-writers, I might not have had the courage to completely voice all the words I wanted to. Because of you sweet people, I did. And watch out...there's more to come!

And to you, my friend. I wish you happiness. Together, we can bring unity to our Earth.

The Audition

THE GAMUT – #1

I am just as comfortable keeping company with a cement truck driver who performs drag in the evening as I was shaking hands with Hillary Rodham Clinton at a business woman's luncheon (although I must say the drag queen had nicer shoes). I am painfully aware of how it feels to talk myself into clinging desperately to a relationship that brings me down, and I know the ultimate exhilaration of the intimate love and protection of a true partner. I know from personal experience the difference between a drug high and a life high. I know how it feels to have lost a father before death took him, yet I also know the triumph of joining together right before he died. I know how it feels to grow up hating an older sister and then to grow closer to one another as adults and become the best of friends. I know the unlimited, unconditional love of a mother…period.

I know how to wrestle a midget in lime Jell-O and I…well…I guess there's really nothing I can compare to that one. I know how it feels to steal and how it feels to be stolen from. I know how it feels to live with an eating disorder every day of my life. I know how it feels to hate myself; but I also know how it feels to respect, love, and honor myself. I know how it feels to keep lugging around baggage and how it feels to finally let it go. Through self-confidence, I have accomplished much—yet there were times when I withered in the face of overwhelming insecurities. I've often felt despair and nothing-ness, only later to discover a puffy, white cloud that I know was placed in the sky for just me to enjoy. I've pawned jewelry to buy drugs and alcohol, rolled quarters (and sometimes nickels) to pay rent, and I've paid $900 a night to romp around in a five-star resort with the love of my life. I know the certainty and endless wonderment of believing passionately in my spirituality, yet I still have doubts which cause me to try and rationalize it away. I know how to dream.

I want to keep adding to my list.

DAHLING! DON'T TELL ME WHERE YOU KEEP YOUR BRUSH!

"Mommy, why does Uncle Robert have boyfriends instead of girlfriends?" I couldn't have been more than four years old when I asked my mother that question about her younger brother who would have been twenty-six years old at the time. Mom smiled tenderly, knelt down to my level, cupped my face in her hands, and gave me an uncomplicated and honest answer. "Carol" she said, "all of your life you will meet boys who like boys and girls who like girls. It's not bad, it's not different—it's just the way it is."

Even as a child, I was fascinated by my world-renowned interior designer uncle and his environment. His apartment was alive and bold with color, enhanced with big, fresh flower arrangements and always full of people I thought were fake—but fun. Uncle Robert was eccentric, exhilarating, and flamboyant. No one worked a room like my Uncle Robert. Subtly dramatic, he'd incorporate every body part as a prop when he walked, sat down, or told a story—he was a one-man show. Being with Uncle Robert was to be in the eye of a tornado of lavish activities.

His speech was slow, clear, and steady—elaborately laid back—and spiked with intelligent sarcasm. One time in my twenties when I was visiting him, Uncle Robert watched as I withdrew a tube of lipstick from my bra and applied some to my lips. He asked me why I kept makeup in my undergarments. I told him I didn't carry a purse and so I had to keep my money and lipstick in my bra. He paused a moment and then in the verbal-masque of Zsa Zsa Gabor replied languidly, "*Dahling*! Then please don't tell me where you keep your brush!"

Although Uncle Robert was world-traveled, to him there was no place to live other than Manhattan. He worshipped and loved the pulse of his city. Whenever I visited, he rolled out the red carpet and treated me to the incredible entertainment that his city offered. He took me to countless Broadway shows and to social gatherings that were featured in *Town & Country*, *Harper's Bazaar*, and *Architectural Digest*. I rode in stretch limousines, dined at the finest restaurants, and hobnobbed with the glitterati of the world's most cosmopolitan city. On several different occasions, Robert took my sister

Nancy and me to Studio 54 when it was in its heyday, and we never had to wait in line to get in. For a while, he had a time-share on a summer home next to Calvin Klein's cottage on Fire Island. It was on that island when I was about fourteen that I went to my first gay tea dance.

But I always wondered if he did all that for me because he liked me or because he felt he had to or because he perhaps felt that was all he had to give. Although I devoured it, I longed for an emotional bond.

Robert was physically touchy. He loved holding hands and he would clasp my arm in his while strolling and whisper tidbits of information in my ear. I felt privileged yet intimidated because I never knew what to say. Something kept me apart from him, as if there were a transparent partition between us. His world was a total fantasy that I loved to be included in every so often but never wanted for myself. It was too much, too posh, too unrealistic, too rushed, too unfeeling, too cold. When people in his sphere greeted one another, they kissed the air barely allowing their cheeks to touch, and they didn't hug. Although Uncle Robert surrounded himself with people and immersed himself in a world where he was rarely alone, I always sensed that he was lonely.

When it came to material things, Robert was unbelievably generous. It was his heart that he couldn't seem to share. He never left an emotional opening through which anyone could enter. While Robert could love, he allowed himself to be loved in return only to a certain point. Maybe he was afraid to love too much. Maybe it was a defense mechanism since so many people wanted something from him since he'd made it to the top. Everything he did for others was on his time, done his way. Uncle Robert called the shots.

As he got older, he wanted our mother around him. He treated her to several trips to Europe when he had business there and often flew her from her home in Arizona to Manhattan for visits. After my sister and I were grown and on our own, he urged Mom to move to New York and work for him. At that point in his career, he thought of dealing with people as being "a pain in the ass." He felt he was too busy and too important to be pestered by whiny, demanding clients and he knew Mom could handle them with diplomacy and tact and smooth out any bumps that arose. Besides, she was a lovely and convenient escort for the endless affairs he was required to attend. He couldn't understand why Mom chose to stay home and care for her ailing husband. "Why do you want such a boring nursemaid life?" he asked with a noticeable lack of compassion. "Your life is a waste." Robert equated significance in life to fame, wealth, and being the interior designer unparalleled in the world.

Robert's boyfriend Werner was tall, handsome, soft-spoken with a sexy German accent, and gentle and masculine at the same time. I liked him, but I always had the impression that he followed Robert's leads. When Werner died from AIDS-related complications in 1990, Robert told his clients, his friends, and Mom that Werner had died from lung cancer. In fact, at the start of Werner's languishing health, he informed Mom that he and Werner had broken up. Robert was trying to cover up the situation so she wouldn't ask to see him while she was in Manhattan. When Werner was diagnosed, Uncle Robert was tested and found out that he, too, was HIV positive. For years, he kept it to himself. Mom had a clue—as we all did—and she finally asked him point-blank. Robert said no. When at last he did tell her, he asked her to keep it to herself. He didn't want anyone knowing the truth for fear his client base would dwindle and that his friends would drop out of sight. He told Mom, "Who wants a decorator with AIDS?" I don't think Robert ever gave people the chance.

In November 1994, he took Mom with him on his last trip to Europe. Although Robert had been fighting AIDS with exercise, diet, and drug therapy, it was insidiously taking ownership of his body. He held onto Mom's shoulder for support and continued to proclaim his health to the world by wearing layers of clothing in an attempt to conceal his declining weight. While there, he went to the best Italian tailors to procure an entire new wardrobe. He applied makeup to bring color to his skin and to hide the lesions. But his façade fooled no one.

Mom felt the startled stares and heard the whispers within each group they passed. Maybe Robert didn't hear them and actually believed that nobody caught on or maybe, for his own survival and dignity, he wouldn't allow himself to hear them. However, perhaps he heard every one of them.

When Uncle Robert returned to the States, he immediately checked himself into the hospital but refused to stay in the AIDS wing. He died in December 1994. It wasn't until recently that my eyes opened to the fact that Robert gave me so much more than just expensive dinners, Broadway shows, and celebrity connections. Uncle Robert subtly but importantly added to the development and decoration of *my* "interior." From the beginning of me, Robert helped me grow. It's possible that all he felt he had to give and all that I wanted were money and material things. So whether he ever knew it or not, he helped open my world to so much more.

Robert Howard Metzger
October 1, 1939 – December 15, 1994

A LESSON NOT LEARNED

When I was a kid, I destroyed everything. Jewelry, dolls, games, clothes—whatever made its way into my hands, I chewed on it or otherwise mangled it beyond recognition, sending it to a premature death. I once devoured an entire book. I mean devoured it. I ate every page. Poor *Curious George* didn't stay curious for long around me. He, too, was eaten. My parents called me (lovingly, I hope) "Instant Disaster" because of my penchant for ruining things.

When I was in the second grade, I walked home one afternoon and entered our house. "Carol!" my mother shrieked. "Where is your jumper?"

I stood there in my patent leather buckle shoes, white leotards that were ripped at the knees, and a white but soiled turtleneck. Until she pointed out that I wasn't fully dressed, I actually hadn't noticed. I was as surprised as she was, for we both remembered I'd been wearing a jumper that morning. She walked me across the street to the school, looking on the sidewalks and on the playground and in the halls. Alas, no plaid jumper was to be found. She said she was amazed that not a single teacher had remarked to me about my outfit...or lack thereof. To this day, I still have no idea where it went.

The following winter, my parents bought me a faux fur brown coat with a matching hat. I loved them! I felt like a big girl because this coat didn't have clip-on mittens. They'd wanted to buy me a coat with a hood because they knew how I was about things. I begged and promised, however, that I would be extra careful and not lose the hat. I especially loved the big furry pom-poms that were on the ends of the hat's ties.

One day, my father came home from work and called me

downstairs from playing in my room. He bent down and hugged me and asked if I would model my new coat and hat for him. I galloped up the stairs two steps at a time, excited to show off for my daddy. I quickly put on the coat, but I couldn't find the hat anywhere. I looked under my bed and in the closet, but it was nowhere to be found. Maybe he wouldn't notice if I didn't wear the hat.

I flew downstairs and then slowly sauntered and twirled around as if on a fashion runway, posing and smiling and modeling my new coat. My father kept telling me how pretty I looked. Then he said he wanted me to model the hat, too.

"No, Daddy, I just want to show you the coat. Just look at the coat on me!" I started sashaying around in the hallway using every ounce of my cuteness as I tried to distract him from thinking about the missing hat. He was giggling and I loved it because he was laughing and playing with me. We went around a couple of times about the hat and then he abruptly stopped laughing and slapped me hard on the face. I was wholly bewildered! I had no idea why he'd done that. My mother didn't understand either. The instant he hit me, she started screaming at him. "Mike! What are you doing? What are you doing?!"

I still remember the look on her face. I think she was even more shocked than I was. All I could do was stand there holding my hand to my burning cheek and cry. Then my father reached into his coat pocket and drew out my new hat that he'd found lying in the street. "Maybe now you'll learn not to be careless and lose things," he said sternly.

I'm a grown woman now and I still lose things. But what my father tried to teach me that day was a lesson in responsibility.

What I learned, however, was not to trust him, because even his laughter hurt.

THE MAYOR OF NEWKIRK AVENUE

I've always talked constantly. Growing up in my Brooklyn neighborhood, I was known as the Mayor of Newkirk Avenue. Even in kindergarten, I was constantly ordered to be quiet. I rebelled by making up outrageous stories, by being the class clown, and by not following directions. Man, did I hate school! They told me what to do, where to sit, what to draw, and what to think—or at least they tried to. They wanted to wrap regulations around my five-year-old spirit and squeeze the offbeat rhythms and colors out of me. My parents got a good dose of my probable school future when they began getting frequent calls from my kindergarten teacher informing them of my not-for-credit activities.

Throughout elementary school, I was an average student receiving mostly B's and C's (and some below) on my report card. With an insatiable need to be noticed and cursed by a short attention span, I wanted to rule the class. That tested many a teacher's patience and always got me into trouble. In the third grade, I wrapped my arm up in a bandage from wrist to elbow and told my teacher that I had a sprain and wasn't able to write. All I wanted was for everyone to look at me and to ask me what was wrong. Stupid move. I pulled my bandage stunt during the week of the parent-teacher conferences, and so my parents quickly found out.

In 1971, the Sherman clan moved from New York to Arizona. Because my dad had multiple sclerosis, his doctors had urged him to live in a less humid climate. He chose

Tucson. From the first day of school, I was a well-known figure about campus. Everyone knew who I was and I knew
them. I was the only one like me—the mostly tolerated and
accepted school jester, the kid everyone counted on to perform
daredevil acts. I think the teachers let me get away with little
lies and stupid stunts simply because they didn't know how to
handle me. By the sixth grade, I had made up so many wild
stories that even I had a difficult time distinguishing reality
from fantasy. To me, the truth just wasn't full enough or
fun enough.

Mrs. Kathleen Jaccaud, my sixth grade teacher, was one of
my favorites. She was the kind of teacher who had a need to
teach and who had an innate gift for holding a child's attention
without force. Unlike the way I could with all the other teachers, I couldn't talk my way out of homework or work up a
good excuse with her. She took no garbage from me. She was
stern but also compassionate. Mrs. Jaccaud kept in close contact with my parents, giving them updates on my progresses
(and my lack thereof). She was interested in me and talked
with me, not at me. When she asked me about my feelings and
emotions, however, I didn't know what to tell her.

The sixth grade was the year my best friend Buffy fell off
the monkey bars and broke both of her arms. I was so jealous
of the attention and cards and candy and flowers she received
that I became determined to break my own arm. I used my
lunch money to pay Tommy Baldwin, the biggest boy in
school, to fracture my right fin. We tried a couple of methods,
but neither worked. Then Tommy told me to sit in a chair and
put my arm over the back of it. He ran towards me with all his
might and pushed me over, making the chair and my body
weight crash on my arm. We did this at recess in front of an

audience in the classroom, and Mrs. Jaccaud walked in at the core of the performance. I could tell by the look on her face that she was upset with me. She told me to stay after class so she could talk with me privately.

"What is so bad that makes you want to break your arm?" she asked. I didn't have an answer for my favorite teacher. By the time the school bus dropped me off at home, she had phoned Mom and Dad and suggested that I talk to the children's school counselor in the district. They agreed that maybe some intervention might help calm me down and focus on what's going on inside.

The counselor came to my school and I was thrilled that the sessions got me out of class. I especially loved the fact that students noted something special was happening to me. Being put under a microscope was as good as being in the radiance of a spotlight. The counselor asked me questions about emotions and feelings, but I didn't know what to tell her either. I knew I didn't like being punished all of the time. I didn't like being called a liar. I didn't like crying and being constantly confused and angry with myself. Although always aware that I would get in trouble as my shenanigans unfolded, I had an overwhelming need to run with them to see how far I could go. It was as if my actions and my thoughts were not mine at all. I didn't feel anything inside. My world was all make-believe. The more she studied me, the more the stories kept rolling, piling up like smashed cars in an accident on a highway. I couldn't stop myself.

In the eighth grade, I wanted my period so badly that I bit the insides of my cheeks until they bled, and then I spit the blood out onto a sanitary napkin. I honestly thought that if I *pretended* hard enough, I would begin to menstruate. I even talked myself into feeling stomach cramps. I came apart and fessed up when Mom showed me how to use one of those old fashioned belts. She was troubled, to say the least, about the lengths I would go to get center stage.

That same year, an announcement came over the school's public address system that my favorite math teacher had died. He'd been the favorite of many of the students and many of them started crying. I started crying, too. As I sat on the brick wall next to Buffy I thought, *am I upset because everyone else is, or because I'm getting attention, or do I really feel sad about his death?* I couldn't feel my feelings. I was at a loss with myself because I felt so empty.

THE START OF A LONG SCHLEPP

Although I never cared to work, it was a necessity in the Sherman house. Dad pushed both my older sister Nancy and me out of the birthing box as soon as the milk dried on our chins. But even so, I've always (well, in most cases) been a good hired hand (at least in my later years). I come from a strong Jewish lineage of hardy work ethic and suffering.

I was thirteen years old when I got my first job. It was with a lady who owned a dog kennel where she bred German shepherds. I earned $1.50 an hour and worked three hours on Saturdays and another three hours on Sunday picking ticks off shepherd pups and drowning them in a jar of turpentine tar. (The ticks, not the pups.) I also cleaned the kennels, but the best part of the job I saved for the last hour of my workday. It was playing with the puppies. I was told this was important to get the dogs integrated with society. I didn't give a hoot about that. I would have paid to play with the pups.

The owner was a hunched-over woman in her sixties, with mounds of flesh protruding from her upper back and veins the size of sipping-straws sticking out of her harsh, chapped hands. She had scraggly, mistreated, hair that she sometimes wore in uneven pigtails. She was a walking "fashion don't" who commingled striped polyester shorts with plaid flannel shirts. This woman talked to herself more than she talked to me. I knew she was tempting me into a conversation when she told me that she "loved the smell of dogs in heat." I also received one employee benefit: free lunch. Usually it was a bologna sandwich, but sometimes it was a black bean burrito that smelled like the ticks from the turpentine jar. Being that Mom spent more money in gas taking me back and forth each weekend than I would have netted in a year, I was forced to look for employment elsewhere after about three months.

From the kennel, I went to Food Giant, a small neighborhood market about half-mile from our home on the outskirts of Tucson. I bagged groceries and cleaned up spilled foodstuffs ("broken profits" as Hobart, the manager, called them) in the aisles. My responsible sister Nancy had held this important position before me, so they hired me on the basis of her good name alone. Six months after they hired me, however, they bagged me. All I did was keep asking for weekends off. The problem was, I only worked weekends. Second job... first termination.

Then, when I was fifteen, I was forced to work on weekend mornings assisting the live-ins at a nursing home with their art class. I had fun doing that, but actually I didn't get paid for it. It was the community service work I had to do after being arrested for shoplifting during a fantasy-shopping extravaganza when I pretended to be some sort of con artist ripping off the rich—a bad-girl *Charlie's Angels*. But after I was apprehended and forced to face reality, I was given a choice of cleaning up the highway or working in a nursing home. I chose the elders and they loved me! We'd make clay pots in between our singing and laughing. They even asked me to stay on after my sentence was up, but I didn't want to. My heart crashed each Saturday morning to find a pot dried and ready to be painted, only to hear that the person who made it had died during the week. I learned very quickly to stop asking, "Where's Martha or Fred or Helen…"

SCHOOL DAZE, SCHOOL HAZE

High school was the worst. The jump from eighth grade to ninth wrecked me. My grades were lower in high school than they had been in any other grade, and they plummeted further every year. In addition to hating the place, I stayed stoned the entire time. For me, it really was *high* school. I learned about marijuana from a fellow freshman and began to partake on a regular basis. I belonged to a carpool with the naughty kids in the subdivision and we'd roll cigar-sized joints at 7:30 every morning.

The only good things about high school were the many other "outside" kids like me and the different cultures and lifestyles. The elementary and junior high schools Nancy and I had attended had few minorities, low-income families, or one-parent households. High school was a different ball game. There I rubbed shoulders daily with Mexicans, Indians, and African-American kids. I met kids with alcoholic parents, a handful of "out" gay students, teenage girls with babies, and students who had to hold a job to help their moms pay rent. It made me realize the smallness of my own world.

I made friends with Marcy. Although she was a year younger than I was, she was the one who taught me some street smarts. Her upbringing was completely different from mine. Her parents were divorced, she had no ties with her dad, and her mom worked a lot when Marcy was young, leaving Marcy and her older brother to fend for themselves. Unlike us, she lived in the city, in a small house that didn't have antiques or a chest freezer full of frozen meat in the garage. She shared her house with her brother, her mom, and her mom's boyfriend, Ed. Ed was black. This was the first time I'd ever seen an interracial couple. I thought it quite cool and found myself staring at her mom's and Ed's hands when they were clasped. It was if their hands were literally hugging the difference in colors.

Marcy was with me during a lunch break from school the first time I mixed alcohol and Valium. My next class required me to assist mentally challenged students with schoolwork (my guidance counselor hoped my helping others would raise my sense of self-worth), but all I remember was stumbling out of the room to get air. The next thing I knew, I was in the nurse's office with my very tense parents waiting for me to open my eyes. It was close to five o'clock in the evening. They knew about the alcohol but not the Valium, and I remember thinking how serious this would be if they knew about the tranquilizer. I thought I was lucky, though I was suspended from school for a week and punished by my parents. Mom begged me to open up and let her in, but I pushed her away. She had always been my life preserver, but I wasn't swimming to her anymore. Her words, "I'll always love you, Carol, but I don't like you right now," tore through me but, as with Mrs. Jaccaud and the school therapist, I just didn't know what to tell her. I was so unhappy that I couldn't do right by the people I loved and who loved me.

By my junior year, I was into more and more drugs. I had become so angry that I withdrew from any adult who had an ounce of authority and from any students who had it on the ball. The chip on my shoulder was so big I don't know how I fit through doorways. In constant trouble with my teachers, I just about wore a path through the concrete schlepping to the principal's office. Of course, nothing was ever my fault. I was either the victim or I was just in the wrong place at the wrong time. The troubles I caused myself up through the eighth grade were quite different from the problems I experienced in high school. When you're younger, you can get away with a lot more. I was in high school and what I was doing wasn't cute and acceptable anymore, and the teachers just didn't want to deal with me.

In my four years at high school, I went to one school dance, never went to a prom, and never joined any of the many clubs. I didn't want anything to do with them. From beginning to end, all I wanted was to leave. I had no place in high school. The school was big into things like technical training, Future Farmers of America, and sports. I didn't take part in any of those. On the other hand, neither was I one of the really bad kids who sold drugs or started fires in the school. By contrast, I was invisible and hated it. This school had more than five hundred students. The safe feeling of community that I had from knowing the same teachers and kids from year to year in junior high was no longer a handle I could hold on to. I got so lost.

FREE AT LAST...WELL, SORT OF

During my senior year, I got a part-time job working in a department store. It was called "Diamonds," but there wasn't any sparkle to it. It was somber, corporate, and lacked any type of humor. The ambiance matched most of the employees' attitudes, for all they did was kvetch about working there. I felt as out of place at Diamonds as I did in school. I also had an urge to steal merchandise, but a policy was enforced making all female employees dump their purse belongings into a see-through-plastic-zippered bag when they clocked in to work. We had to carry that around the store in place of our purses. That kept my fingers to myself. In addition, they hired plainclothes security guards who got righteous kicks from catching employee-thieves. I always felt badly for the ones who were caught. Nevertheless, Diamonds was good for my acting career. I was a floater, which meant they put me wherever they needed someone. One day, I was an expert in men's shoes, the next in vacuum cleaners, and the next in costume jewelry, wigs, or kitchen appliances. Take it from me, people will believe almost anything when they're itchin' to buy something.

In the latter part of my senior year, I learned I was three credit hours short of graduating and that I would have to enroll in summer school and pass those courses in order to get my diploma. I couldn't take any more of school and so I plotted my escape. I took an elective class, working in the high school office as an aide, filing and coding. When the opportunity arose, I seized it. I went into my files and penned in the missing credits. (So many carbon copies, so little time! It's a good thing there weren't any computers then or I would never have been able to execute my plan.)

As I stood in line at the 1979 commencement ceremony anticipating my name being called, I was schvitzing like a swine, expecting the principal, Mr. Sowel—who had rolls of fat in the back of his neck—to yank me out for my ingenious breakout plan. However, I graduated with the rest of the senior class, threw that stupid, square, tasseled cap in the air, and was never questioned.

Directly after sort of graduating from high school, I moved out of my parents' house, found an apartment and a roommate, and enrolled in a large university. Within a month, I simply stopped going. Being a slipped-through-the-cracks high school student left me wholly unprepared and confused in college. My reading skills were poor, I couldn't follow lectures, and the university's classrooms were the size of my high school auditorium. Talk about feeling invisible and stupid. After that failed attempt, Dad suggested I try a smaller school and so the following semester, I enrolled in a community college. Again, I "dis-enrolled" after a month. In mid-term, I gave it another go…and dropped out again. Three school strikeouts in one year. At least I was consistent.

"To Hell with Parmesan Cheese! I'll Have Those!"

Then, for once, I took his advice. I was glad Dad believed college wasn't for everybody and I was thankful he didn't pressure me into torturing myself in school again. He told me that if I wasn't going to stay in school, I needed to get a full-time job and support myself. I left dim Diamonds and got a forty-hour-per-week job as a waitress at Pepe's Pasta Palace in

Tucson, Arizona. This is where my true passion for the culinary arts and for the service industry began. Besides, it was cool having cash tips in my pocket instead of waiting on a paycheck.

Pepe's was dark, dull, dingy, and dismal. Painted paneling covered the walls and the drop ceiling was painted and dusted with glitter à la early 1970s. The carpet was so thick with dirt that I'm convinced, through evolution, it could have sprouted legs and run out by itself. Pepe's smelled old, but not the good kind of old smell that wafted through my grandma's apartment. It was more old + rank = stench. The black vinyl booths were slick with steak grease and spaghetti slop and, if you dared slide your hand between the back of the booth and the seat, I'm sure you would have pulled up part of a lunch from 1946.

Pepito, the proprietor, was a walrus of a man with a pig-like nose and a wandering eye. I swear this eye had a mind of its own. It would dance in the socket—up and down, back and forth. Worse than a carnival ride, you'd get dizzy if your conversation with him lasted more than a minute. His size was intimidating in itself but the man's breathing was so labored that it sounded like a pack of mules hoofing their way up Pike's Peak. I thought he would keel over any second. I was afraid that, because I was the new kid, I'd be the one ordered to pound on his chest and give him mouth-to-snout. Pepito's voice sounded like Marlon Brando in the *Godfather*, especially when he'd say things like, "If ya get a buck a head, kid…doin' good." That's what he said when he hired me. He spoke in broken sentences, preferring to grunt and point, as he ordered all his little servant servers around as if he were king. In fact, he was king—the "King of Cholesterol." Every once in a while, he'd bark out a complete sentence and it was all I could do to not applaud in appreciation of the full use of his vocabulary.

The chef at Pepe's swaggered like a saddle-sore cowboy, was as hairy as a primate, and wore glasses as thick as the windshield on an armored truck. These glasses rested on a face so scarred by acne that it looked like a satellite photo of the surface of the moon. Only the mustache hid some of the craters. The chef…hmmm…what was her name? Oh, yeah, it was Daisy. A sweet and delicate name for a lady who was neither. She was major league butch who carried the biggest, shiniest chain wallet on the planet. Daisy was especially proud that it was "genuine leather" and she made sure you knew she had tooled it herself…most likely with her teeth.

Daisy's prior cooking experience must have been at a boot camp. At the staff meetings before the beginning of my shift, Daisy would inform us about the specials and the preparation of her indelicacies. Servers had to line up single file and as our last name was called for attendance, we would say "PRE-SENT." I don't get why we had shift meetings anyway. How hard is it to explain how the cans of food are opened gently with a can opener and then subtly stirred with tap water to create the delicious gravy that compliments the flaky, gray mashed potatoes?

My first day as a waitress was hairier than Daisy's arms. Never having waited tables before was scary enough, but Pepito—the tuskless mammal—followed the newbies around to make sure they were on the up and up. I got a "four top" (four people at a table). It was a group of polyester leisure-suited businessmen clutching their "valu-pak" coupons for the "two-for-the-price-of-one steak and spaghetti lunch special."

When I brought their lunch to the table, I balanced the tray of grub on my left forearm and hand, then set the plates down with my right. I had been practicing this move in the privacy of my own apartment because, in all truth, I am as graceful as a moose. As I bent down over the tray to put the second-to-last business boy's lunch in front of him, I felt something warm and smushy on my bazoombas. Slowly raising up, I looked down at my new white blouse and saw strands of spaghetti dangling from my two tomato-sauced assets while one of the leisure suit boys yelled—just to be sure he got the entire restaurant's attention, "To hell with parmesan cheese! I'll have those!"

That was the first table I'd ever waited on and already I'd started my new career off on the wrong part of my body. I would have preferred not having semolina wheat hanging from my tatalas, but laughing at it is what my darling mother refers to as "making the best of the situation." And that's what I did. I laughed with 'em. I looked over at my fat-man-boss who was rubbing his temples with his knockwurst fingers as his eyes (well, one of them at least) looked up at the dropped-glittered heavens of a ceiling. Content to hear laughter permeate the cave, I was confident that Pepito wasn't going to scrap me, and I was quite tickled to find that the business boys left me a crisp ten spot…and a phone number.

NICHE

I loved having all eyes on me. Always—whether I was five years old playing the lead in Brooklyn's PS 152 kindergarten show the "Little Red Hen" (I sang, "Cluck, cluck, cluck, ca-dag-it") or at fourteen at the high school pep rally squawking and gobbling over a Mr. Microphone when elected "Freshman Class Turkey of 1975." Those are my two shining moments in all of school (besides, of course, forging my high school escape), but I especially liked it when they chose me head turkey. Out of a 120 ninth-graders, they picked me! My dean's list and sorority-bound senior sister was horrified about the eccentric poultry exhibition I performed while she sat in the auditorium with her peers, the entire faculty, and the other five hundred students of high school, but I was glad to have been noticed! Therefore, at nineteen years of age when I simulated a plate of pasta, I was center stage and thrilled.

Working in restaurants. I'd finally found something I was good at. As long as guests would listen, I loved being their personal floor show. I sought out places that needed evening help because I've always been a night person and I love sleeping in. (Mom said when I was a kid, I hated to go to bed for fear I would miss something.) Not being shackled to a desk or confined behind a counter was superb for a person like me, a person born in perpetual motion but with a short attention span. And I loved the constant variety. In a restaurant, I wasn't working with the same people night in and night out—every shift brought new customers and new personalities.

After three or four months, I left Pepe's in search of a restaurant where I could make more money (or, at least a place where the food matched my uniform). I went to work in a new country club, and I made some friends with fellow employees. But as there was very little money to be made as a cocktail waitress in the country club's lounge, I justified stealing to make up for the lack of tips as if the money had been owed to me. Just like four years before when I was busted for shoplifting, it wasn't my fault that I didn't have any money when I wanted those earrings, the roll-on lip gloss, the music books, the Elton John album. So I simply took them. No different at the club where I helped myself to a complete set of dishes for four, along with silverware (including butter knives and shrimp forks), and then later managed to run from the foyer through the parking lot out to my car with a six-foot brass coat stand—and all this in just one night.

Trying to supplement my income, I got a weekend job through a friend I'd met at the club. This second job entailed working for his mom who owned an insurance company. A dispatcher I am not, but pretended to be during the interview. The office was closed on the weekends and customers would call for a particular agent and my responsibility was to put the call through to the agent's home. I somehow managed to disconnect nearly every incoming call. As a result, I was disconnected from the company after just three weekends. I was almost relieved to be let go because the job was terribly tiresome and besides nabbing a glass paperweight from an agent's desk, the place was nearly pillage-proof. I mean, how many packets of coffee and saccharin could I possibly have used?

Apart from the stealing, the restaurant business posed a few other problems for me. Drugs of all varieties are quite accessible in that line of work. Magic mushrooms, Lemon 714s, prescription drugs—anything I wanted to try. Some coworkers were walking drug smorgasbords and I lined up for the buffet. Common practice after shifts was gathering with comrades at a bar to spend the cash tips that were burning a hole in my pocket. Then, of course, there were those after-hour parties at peoples' homes that continued to early morning and sometimes early afternoon. Non-stop parties and bars were my life.

My mom knew there was trouble. I was as lost out of school as in. She had seen me jump from job to job, apartment to apartment, and botch through an entire playbill of room-mates in a short period of time. I quit the activities that I loved: playing the piano, writing music, singing, and appearing with her in community theatre shows. The shows used to be our thing. But it was the same "song" I had sung in school, believing that nothing was ever my fault and that I was purely a victim. Mom had a sense of what was going on. Even when I tried to ignore her, she managed to wriggle her way into my head. Her guidance was persistent. Mom may not have always believed me, but she always believed in me.

Sometimes it's not easy for a weed to grow.

BED ROULETTE

Looking for love in all the wrong places. I'm sure you know the song. Some of us, however, have heard it too much. I know I did. There were times in my life I was quite promiscuous. Dangerously promiscuous. It's nothing I'm proud of, but nei-ther do I beat myself up because of it. It just was.

The first time I had sex was with some guy I picked up in a bar. I'd rather the boy had been a companion, a confidant, or someone I cherished and trusted, but I didn't have that. Besides the transient crushes and several two-week liaisons, I didn't have boyfriends. When talking with friends who share indiscriminate experiences, I'm envious to find that some enjoyed their sexually spirited young adulthood. I didn't. At first it was a novelty having some power and watching boys do the mating-dance to get what they wanted. Sometimes I'd be sent the gift of a good hugger—which is all I really wanted anyway. I have few good memories of the actual sex acts because I didn't like that part. I felt numbly sad when it began because that meant the flirtatious, playful coupling between the boy and me had ended. He was done and didn't need to delude me anymore. He had won. But I thought that's what I had to go through to be loved. I hated the tidal wave of my feelings that followed their finish. Rejected. More alone. Insufficient. I felt I was being pilfered from. Worse, I watched with my eyes wide open while solicited intruders filched bits and pieces of my undeveloped soul.

As I look back with a clearer brain, I realize sex wasn't the reason I was having intercourse. I thought my body was all I had to offer. Unfortunately, many women feel this way. It seems as if we put ourselves second in a desperate attempt to get closer to someone…to anyone. I didn't even know what I had in self-inventory to bring into a relationship, but I knew I wanted to give of myself in much more than just a sexual way, but I didn't know how. I was crying out to be accepted, loved, and held. Those things never materialized from sleeping around.

Sex was something I thought I had to do to become more sophisticated, more womanly, more desirable. In spite of my adolescent behavior, I didn't start having sex until I was eighteen. After that, going to bars, drinking, and bed-roulette quickly became normal behavior for me. I never had sex without getting smashed first, and I continued that orbit for years. Many boys acted as if they were looking for something other than a tumble and I'd blind myself into believing them. Even if the recipient wasn't all that I wanted, I'd talk myself into accepting him "as is," figuring that maybe I'd somehow feel a connection. I would pray, "Please let this be the one." I acted out this scene for each willing but unwitting actor. The Universe must really have imperial plans for me, because it's a

miracle that I wasn't sliced, diced, and left in an alley somewhere. I am also blessed because I never caught anything that
I couldn't get rid of with a red-faced visit to the drugstore.

I found this poem in an old diary. As crude and trite as it
is, it summed up my feelings at that time. I wrote it in 1981
when I was twenty—about two years after I became sexually
active.

> *I don't need your "love" for a night,*
> *It's just physical attraction.*
> *My mind needs more stimulation*
> *Than just a moment of passion.*
> *Can't fool me, can't fool yourself.*
> *So put those macho-bullshit lines on the shelf.*
> *Your sweet, meaningless words can't get to me anymore.*
> *Don't you dare beg for me,*
> *Don't say you'll give me security,*
> *Because with the dawn you will leave.*
> *And those promises you've made to me,*
> *All will fade, they'll blow away.*
> *Tomorrow's just another day,*
> *From the dignity I've lost,*
> *The truth I've gained.*
> *'Cause all you men are all the same.*

If I knew the score, why did I continue to play the game?
Mom always said, "Nobody's going to love you, Carol, until
you love yourself," and I'd think that was stupid because she
loves me, my friends love me, my customers love me, and other
people love me. What does she mean by loving myself? It
sounded silly. Then she'd follow that up with, "Why do you

think so little of yourself that you always wind up in bad way?" At that time, I couldn't comprehend that I ever put myself in hurtful situations. Instead, I thought everything worked against me.

As I reflect on that era with the benefit of an accumulated twenty years of wisdom, I realize that I made my life more difficult than it had to be. I was not born a victim. I created that role for me to perform because I hadn't the love, respect, or self-motivation to progress into a good light. I set myself up for disappointments and trauma with the eons of "woe is me, I can't do anything right" and "why do bad things always happen to me?" It wasn't until much later that I realized it took me to move beyond and get out of these so-called "victim" circumstances.

With Mom's voice echoing faintly in the background, I did move beyond the drugs, the destructive behavior, and the self-mutilation of my soul. Because of Mom's words, not only did I make it through those times, I think I made it through damned well!

No one is going to love you Carol, until you love yourself!
It's not silly. I understand now.

YOU WON'T FIND THIS JOB IN THE CLASSIFIEDS

After four months at the country club, I still wasn't making any money. So when there was nothing left for me to steal, I booked it out of there and stumbled upon my favorite career opportunity in Tucson. I was lucky enough to meet up with an entrepreneur named Dickster (I actually believe that was his birth name!) who offered me a great — but, as he made it abundantly clear — temporary opportunity. Regardless, it wouldn't have taken much to have a longer run than most of my positions up to that point.

I was between roommates, and there was no friend's dwelling available where I could flop for a while, and so I was back at my parents' house. Mom and Dad believed I worked in an office of some kind. Every Monday through Friday, my alarm clock would sound at 7:30 A.M. I loved this job, so I would leap out of bed and dress myself in work clothes similar to those a secretary would wear, including hose, dress, nice shoes, etc. Within an hour, I was racing down the street in my mufflerless Pinto to Dickster's residence.

Dickster had the shoulders of a linebacker, was really hairy, and had a Fu Manchu mustache that he sometimes knotted at the ends with colored beads. He was in his mid-twenties and though he may have looked like a man, he was but a boy, the type of kid who loved to laugh after passing some gas. Dickster was devoid of manners in every way, especially when eating, and he also felt the freedom to scratch and rearrange his genitals through his pants in front of anybody. The small apartment that Dickster rented was illuminated with neon beer signs, decorated with naked-girl posters, and trashed with athletic socks, jock straps, protective sports gear, beer cans, and empty to-go containers from fast-food restaurants. It looked like a fraternity house had thrown up. But he was loud, raunchy, fun, and was fond of telling politically incorrect jokes. For the record, Dickster and I were just friends.

Upon arriving at Dickster's, I would strip off my costume and throw on a pair of jeans and a T-shirt. Sitting in front of a TV and on the floor with my back resting against a couch, I covered my lap with a white, plastic garbage bag. On top of that, I angled a window screen and was at last in work-position to clean kilos of marijuana and then to roll joints. I was always the favorite roller in the carpool in high school, so I had lots of practice, which made my résumé for Dickster look quite good. Remember the times you'd go to a concert and people would peddle joints for a buck or two? If you bought a joint at a concert in Arizona during 1981, I most likely rolled it. At noon, I'd stretch my arms and legs (especially my fingers) and stand up. Dickster gave me a full hour for lunch, which he paid for and brought to me. Then I would resume rolling until the standard five o'clock quitting time when I would scrub my hands with Ajax to clean the resin from my fingertips, put my secretary garments back on, and drive home high.

Although being a secretary isn't usually strenuous labor, Mom always wondered why I came in so hungry. The pay was $25 per day and a handful of joints. Easy, no hassles, no employment papers to fiddle with, banker's hours to boot, plus Dickster had cable TV. Never did I call in sick or ask for a day off. I had a perfect attendance record, but after four months of employment with Dickster, Inc., he no longer needed my expertise, and I was laid off. Note I was not fired. Dickster terminated my position. He drifted to other opportunities and for a while, I just drifted, too.

A FRIEND OF THE FAMILY

Drifting…drifting…drifting. Eventually, I washed up on the shores into the loving care of a special lady. Sharon was one of the many life jackets the Universe has thrown to me over my lifetime so that someone was always there to scoop me up from the wayward waves.

I first met Sharon when her husband was commissioned by my parents to build a rock fireplace in their home. She was ten years older than I was, and though she was an extrovert, she didn't have many friends. I think she gave up a lot of herself when she got married. She'd been a wild child of the sixties and had done her fair share of partying and putting her parents through hell. Through her experiences, she understood how screwed-up young people could still evolve into good adults. She was honest, homespun, responsible, and had a sense of self. Because of her own experiences, Sharon quickly recognized that I had neither love nor respect for myself.

I told Sharon about everything except my theft problems. She knew about the drugs, the bed-hopping, and the trouble I had with Dad. She never judged him or me; she just listened and sometimes offered suggestions. She'd remind me that my father was handed a bad deal with his multiple sclerosis and how that could make him nasty and isolated and leave him with a terrible attitude towards life.

Sharon and her husband opened a small pizzeria called Oceans of Pizza on the east side of Tucson. I worked for them for a short while after my joint-rolling stint at Dickster's. Their business didn't make it, nor for that matter did their marriage. After their breakup, Sharon moved into an apartment with her baby and asked if I'd be interested in moving in with her. She was looking for help with her child and for companionship for herself during that difficult and lonely time. My mother liked Sharon a lot and was relieved that I was moving in with her. She knew I was in good hands.

It was a good relationship for both of us. Sharon was a nurturing person and needed to be needed, especially then, and I needed to be taken care of. She fed me, provided a roof over my head, and drove me to and from whatever job I held at the moment. She provided much more than these material things, however; but I didn't realize *how* much until years later.

THE MIDGETS IN MY LIFE – #1

After Ocean's of Pizza sank, I went to work at a small record and tape store. For once, I actually put some thought into this rung of my employment ladder. I'd always loved music and had been toying with the idea of becoming a DJ for a radio station. The notion of getting paid to talk energized me, so I decided to learn all I could about music. I was employed at the record store for a good six months but unfortunately, an accomplice and I stole so much merchandise that we may have been why the shop went out of business.

Next, I worked at a car stereo shop where I swabbed the insides of eight-track and cassette players with long, wooden Q-Tips soaked in alcohol. Joe, the owner, told me this process was the "preparation stage" for getting the machines ready for him to repair, except for the fact that he never fixed them. He barely came around because he was so strung out on cocaine. "Just tell 'em their crap is fine and charge thirty bucks." What a disaster! Customers came back so angry and frustrated that they yelled at me like I was an IRS agent insisting that they owed an overdue penalty fee that they really didn't owe. Joe always wanted to pay me in coke, but that was one drug I never cared for. I insisted on cash. Within a month of my employment, the shop closed owing me money. The day I found out I was about to hop on the job carrousel again, I went to drown my sorrows at a scrungy bar that I frequented.

I wanted to see the routine show of male strippers, but they weren't on the agenda that night. Instead, the entertainment was a mixture of alcohol-induced lounge lizards, a couple of midgets, and a kiddie swimming pool filled with lime Jell-O. Voilà! Midget Jell-O wrestling!

The first prize was $150. I hadn't made a hundred and fifty smackers in the past four weeks! I was supposed to be helping Sharon with the rent which was nearly due, but now I was out of a job.

Besides socking a schoolmate in elementary school, I've never been a fighter or even a very confrontational person. But still, just how hard could it be wrestling a midget? I figured that I was in the right place at the right time. I felt it was destiny. Perhaps this was my new vocation! At that point in my years, I'd done a lot more for a lot less. Plus, I was always tingling for a little adventure. I volunteered to wrestle and was given a pair of shorts and a T-shirt to wear for the wrestling match. I mean, it wasn't like I was naked or anything, for heaven's sakes.

Before I could say jumbo shrimp, I found myself in the pool opposite a hobbit. Funny, but at the time, it didn't seem that odd. My opponent's name was Stud. I can't remember the names of half the men I've bedded, but I can remember the name of the yardstick I wrestled in Jell-O. The only instruction I got was that mostly anything was okay except hair pulling and tossing the midget into the air and out of the slimy green sludge. Midgets, I was told, had to stay close to the ground. I won't touch that one…it's too easy.

The bell clanged for the round to begin and Stud ran towards me at full force, bounced into the air like a sawed-off mattress spring, and wrapped his fire hydrant legs around my waist. That was the moment I realized this was deranged, especially with the crowd screaming and laying bets. Even in my shock, I pictured a fat king roosting on his throne and laughing as he threw the half-chewed bones of animals over his shoulder. But Stud seemed to really enjoy this exploited circus. Each time he leapt at me with fervor, he buried his head in my sticky, Jell-O'd chest.

I was certain that he had done this before.

As the Jell-O squished between my toes, I tried to suppress my growing feelings of anger. After all, it didn't seem proper to brawl with this abbreviated man. But then Stud knocked the breath out of me a few times and I really started getting irked. Besides, I needed the money. Right then and there, I decided I wasn't going to let this mini-male get the best of Carol Sherman. Like Rocky Balboa in the last seconds with his opponent Apollo Creed, I cleared the lime Jell-O out of my nostrils, mustered all my reserve strength, and gave poor Stud a wee surprise. I flipped his pygmy-legs out from underneath him, straddled his body, and clamped my hands around his wrists. He was down for the count and I was $150 richer. I even bought Stud a cocktail with my winnings. And to answer the question as to how hard can it be to wrestle a midget? I've never caught a greased pig, but I reckon the sensation is similar.

THE TROUBLE WITH PANTYHOSE – #1

I hate the feel of pantyhose on my legs. I hate the way they suffocate my pores and I hate the way they make me itch. My crotch can't breathe, I feel like a bratwurst when I wear them, and to tell you the truth, I've had some unpleasant experiences due to these non-organic garments. I can't even begin to imagine why drag queens want to wear them...and don't get me started on pumps.

Sharon was taking classes at a community college and it was there that she met a woman named Deidra. When I decided that wrestling midgets in Jell-O wasn't my forte, Deidra introduced me to the owners of a Lebanese restaurant called the Rubiyat who hired me to work as a waitress. Yes, here I was, a nice little twenty-one-year-old Jewish lass working in an Arab restaurant in 1982, smack dab in the middle of the Israeli-Arab territory wars. I never gave it a thought, but I found out some other people did. Mom always told me that people can get along, but nations can't—and she's right. As long as my employers didn't try to claim half my station and tips, everything was cool with me. My new Arab family gave me the Arabic name of Aiysha because, supposedly, she was a goddess with big, brown dancing eyes. I found this terribly charming.

Lebanese know how to cook. Their food springs like a gymnast on every palate—under your tongue, off the insides of your cheeks, and up to the roof of your mouth. It is robust, daring, and satisfies all your taste bud whims, and there's no such thing as "too much" garlic. On delivery days, when the typical restaurant quickly ho-hums while putting supplies away, the Rubiyat first took time to celebrate the arrival and abundance of the food. Both the owners and the staff gathered around a stainless steel table in the kitchen and blessed the food. A brief meditation of your own silently followed. I loved this rich ritual.

After the blessing, the two chubby, dark-haired, male owners began clapping and singing in their native tongue. The middle of the table was dowsed with olive oil, strewn with chopped fresh garlic, hummus, tabbouleh, fresh and dried herbs and spices, and then piled high with cut up veggies and savory raw and cooked meats. The table was absent of plates, and fresh, warm, handmade pita bread served as our forks and our mouths were our napkins. We would lick our fingers clean only to plunge them back into the mounds of the celebrated food for more. It was pure and simple, earthy and uniting. I felt like I belonged. I hadn't had that feeling since performing in the community theatre shows with Mom.

Everyone scooped and talked, giving suggestions on the evening's specials, yakking about the joint in general and joking around with one another. Then the girls cleaned up the mess and put deliveries away, while the guys sat, smoked, and picked their teeth with matches. I didn't love *this* ritual. I understood from the wife of one of the owners that it had taken a while for the men to even allow the women—including their wives—to stand at the table and eat beside them. Welcome to America, boys!

The Rubiyat was a large open space with lots of windows and low tables. Guests sat on plush, tasseled pillows on beautiful, imported rugs. Arabian music paisleyed through the garlic-scented air along with the clamor of pots and pans and loud Middle-eastern language. Yelling was natural between the owners and wives and sometimes they'd be so deep into an argument that I would have to bang my hands on the counter and shout in order to get them to cook my damn orders. "Yálla!" was a word I used to hear in my dreams when I worked at the Rubiyat. They told me it meant "Get this food and deliver it before it gets cold!" I believed them for a while, but in Arabic reality it means "Hurry!" or "Let's go!" Working there was exotic, fun, far from the norm, and what's more, they liked me!

My uniform was a big, simply-decorated, wool caftan, and it was very hot. On a busy Friday evening after escaping to the restroom because my molars had begun to float, I raced back to the dining room trying to remember where I'd left off. In the fog of the anarchy of "who needs what and what food is ready to be delivered where," the entire room began to clap and laugh. Did I miss something when I was in the bathroom? Did someone take one too many puffs off the hookah? I kept pivoting myself in a small circle trying to figure out who or what these people were applauding and laughing at. As a certain coolness came over my entire body, I knew. My caftan was tucked inside the top of my pantyhose in the back. And my pantyhose were nude. And I wasn't wearing underwear. My rear end was smiling to the patrons in the dining room, especially to the young couple sitting on the floor directly behind my behind. I quickly pulled my caftan down and ducked into the kitchen behind the swinging door. As I peeked out of the door's rectangle window, I saw my audience still in stitches and became intoxicated by the laughter of my appreciative public—so I trotted back out for a bow.

Crack doesn't always kill. Sometimes it enhances gratuities.

EVIL CAN BE INTOXICATING

Deidra was a full-blooded American Indian with black eyes that drilled right through you. When light beams met her thick, black hair, rainbow prisms played off her head. Her skin wasn't dark, but ivory. It was the softest skin I'd ever seen, and she took elaborate measures to make sure it stayed that way with creams, lotions, buffers, and saunas. Her nose was sharp, her lips full, and her cheekbones high and sculpted. Deidra was calculatingly saucy, sexy, and alluring, and carefully groomed herself to remain that way. She spent a lot of time on her looks because they were directly linked to her wallet. She was every man's fantasy, every man's desire—and she made the most of it.

For nearly six months, Sharon, Deidra, and I were inseparable. At first, Sharon was impressed with Deidra's poise and strong personality, but quickly caught on that Deidra was a user of humans and knew she was trouble. Sharon tried to get me to see Deidra for what she really was, but I was gripped, charmed, and entranced. As I was empty inside, I was a perfect candidate for Deidra's cult. Anyone with an ounce of self-assuredness could see through Deidra and know instinctively not to get too close. Sharon wasn't the only one. Several other people also told me to avoid Deidra. Even my parents didn't trust her and soon forbade me to let her into their home. I, however, remained blind.

There was a huge blowup between Sharon and Deidra (I still don't know what happened) and in no time, Deidra moved me out of Sharon's place and set me up in another apartment. She paid the deposit and the first month's rent and even found a new roommate for me! Deidra persuaded me that Sharon was "too straight and boring" and that I had no need for her. I remember the terrible feeling I had in the pit of my stomach, a feeling which I now know was my voice telling me this wasn't right. I ignored it, of course. Deidra was more fun to be with.

Deidra paid a great deal of attention to me, something I craved. She supplied me with clothes and makeup, and instructed me on how to groom myself. She invested a lot of time in remodeling me and teaching me how to take pride in my appearance. She took me shopping for clothes, introduced me to expensive salons for haircuts, encouraged me to eat healthier foods, and even took me to my first gynecological visit and got me started on birth control pills. In a scene vaguely reminiscent of *Pygmalion*, she lectured me on table etiquette, including how to hold my glass with feminine style and how to gingerly nibble food on the tip of a fork in a way that would turn a guy on. She drank whiskey straight up with a twist and a soda back, claiming it was far more impressive to order than the cheap Chablis I gulped down. As I had become her mockingbird protégé, I was soon ordering whiskey.

As was I, Deidra was a thief. In fact, I was in cahoots with her on some of her exploits. She was very good at being bad. Like many creatures in the animal kingdom, Deidra would prey on the weak, take what she wanted, and discard the rest without remorse. She'd swoop in and filch from whatever roommate I had (she moved me around three times), quickly ascertaining that they were in situations she could exploit, whether it was a boyfriend, a drug stash, clothes, or money. She was so deft at these crimes that her victims—often confused by drugs and alcohol—rarely caught on to the fact that they were being strung along. Whenever she was accused, she'd use her charms to serpentine her way out of it. If that didn't work, she'd change jobs or move to another city to elude her accusers.

Although life with Deidra was a surreal, dark fantasy, I have to admit it was exciting. I never knew what the next moment would bring. It was as if Deidra were the conniving queen spy and I was her "not-as-smart-but-comedic" sidekick. I wonder now what good I was to her. Perhaps she was more valid if she had a naïve, young, funny girl as her partner. Someone who rounded her edges. Someone who made her more believable. I think she chose me because she needed me, but I didn't know that then. Evil can be very intoxicating and I wasn't strong enough to remain sober.

Deidra liked cocaine and attached herself to others who shared her addiction. She called them her friends, although she would steal from them or sleep with them to get more dust (as they would probably do to her). She slithered her way into the hearts, minds, desk drawers, pants, and homes of coke dealers and heavy users, and worked whomever and whatever she could to get her share.

One night while I was working at the record store, Deidra called from a bar where she'd met a coke dealer. She said this guy's friend was going to pick me up and take me to where she was going to be staying for the weekend. I dutifully obeyed and soon found myself in a house in the poor Hispanic part of Tucson. This small house had a state-of-the-art burglar system, wrought iron bars on all the windows and doors, locks on the inside doors, a gallery of velvet paintings, and was decorated in as many vibrant colors as Disneyland. (Unlike Disneyland, however, there was a small handgun lying on a table by the bolted and latched front door.)

I spent the night in this house but I refused to do any coke because I didn't care for it. More importantly, I didn't want to owe *anything* to *anybody*. I curled up in a red velvet recliner but I didn't sleep a second that night because I was scared out of my gourd. Meanwhile, Deidra partied all night. When she came out of one of the bedrooms at sunrise, I told her I didn't want to stay there another night. I said I wanted to go back to my own apartment. All coked up and red-eyed, Deidra was furious with me for being a baby. She was mad that I didn't do the coke that was offered to me and angry that I wouldn't have sex with the dealer's partner. The dealer must have had at least a small conscience…he took me home.

Deidra stayed away from my apartment for several days and didn't phone. It was then that I finally caught on that *she* needed *me*, that I was important to her. I figured she'd call eventually, and she did.

I knew I had to get away from her, yet at the same time (and I know you're probably not going to understand this), I wanted her approval and for her to be proud of me. Still, I wasn't comfortable staying at the Rubiyat anymore because of her connection with the owners. I decided to move to Phoenix. Dreading the scene where I'd tell her I was leaving, I practiced my lines over and over in my head. Instead of being furious or disappointed, she laughed when I told her. Then she stared right at me and said, "You'll come back to me. I know it."

I had a sick feeling she might be right.

THANKS FOR THE RIDE HOME, SIR!

Late 1982 — My sister Nancy had already moved to Phoenix where she attended Arizona State University, gotten married, and settled down there. Although she and I were now living in the same city, I rarely saw her. It was my choice. She'd call, asking me to go shopping or inviting me to her house, but mostly I stayed to myself. I had done so many wrong things and the trail behind me was so spider-webbed, illogical, and sordid, I had trouble identifying with people. What could I possibly talk to my nice, upper-middle-class, straight-shooter sister about? Getting loaded and waking up in strange places?

Petty theft or worse? Being the lookout for a shaky cocaine heist with Deidra? Sleeping with hundreds of men? Rolling joints for a living? Taking all the gold jewelry that my grandma had left me and pawning it for money for drugs and alcohol? Since I couldn't even relate to myself, I severed all ties with everyone else...everyone but the men I continued to pick up in bars. I was not only alone, but very lonely. And moving away didn't solve my problems, because they followed me.

At least I wasn't as naïve about people (especially men) as I had been before. I lost some of what my grandmother referred to as baby fat, Deidra taught me how to dress, and with her guidance, I cultivated a devilish charm—a flippant, independent, sensual sex-kitten aura that men were immediately attracted to. Although it was a false front and I could play the part well, I couldn't keep it up for long because I didn't feel charming and I wasn't independent and I didn't want sex. Still, I enjoyed playing with the power it gave me over men. I created my persona by copying Deidra, the fantasy women in *Cosmopolitan* magazine, and the vixens in movies and on television. My whole life was a pretense. Worse, I'd become a chronic liar and talked myself into believing my own fiction. No reality. I had advanced very little. I was still the same person as years before when I thought that if I pretended hard enough my period would start.

In Phoenix, I applied for a job at a T.G.I. Fridays. They hired me right away, gave me an employee manual, fitted me for a uniform, and told me I would begin training that week. I was elated! Then the manager dude mentioned that I'd have to take a lie detector test, as all new hires were required to do, and he set it up for later that day. My elation instantly turned into anxiety. The next morning, he called me and said that he'd made a mistake in hiring me, that the restaurant really didn't need any more help. Right. I'd failed the test. I remember how my heart rate tripled when I was asked the question, "Have you ever stolen from a place where you were employed?" When I said that I hadn't, the needle jumped off the paper. I was only twenty-one years old and my past was already catching up to me.

I conceded to sitting behind the desk as a receptionist at a musical instrument store, scheduling work orders and answering phones. I hated it. An older woman in accounts receivable who had worked there since B.C. constantly warned me about getting yeast infections if I continued to wear tight pants. My god, how she annoyed me! She smelled like a wet re-lit cigarette and her face was starting to dry out and her cheeks were concave from all of the drawing and puffing. Her wrinkles birthed wrinkles.

The only good thing about living in Phoenix was that I liked my apartment and my neighbors were cool. I even got a puppy and named him Beau, which was short for rainbow. I love rainbows!

Every Sunday in the Phoenix suburb of Scottsdale, I used to go to a park with Beau. There's a string of art galleries in this park along with quaint cafes, beautiful bronze sculptures, and intricate gardens with fountains. Beau and I spent hours meandering about. Older, wealthy men continually hit on me and while I turned them down, it started me thinking. I slept with men for nothing (and I do mean *nothing*), so why shouldn't I charge? What's so bad about that? I could pick and choose to whom I sold my body, I could control my own hours, *and* I could bring my dog along. I figured that if Deidra could do it for cocaine, I could do it for rent. I decided I would be a high-class call girl. Now there was an aspiration!

Since the owner of the company where I worked constantly made passes at me, I concluded that he was going to be my starting point. Although the thought of sleeping with an unattractive, married, heavy, older man with a hair blanket on his back repulsed me, my intention was to quit my humdrum job and have sex with him once a week for a couple of hundred dollars a pop. I did this with him once and when the degrading twenty minutes were all over and done with, I was mortified about the whole thing. Worse, I didn't know how to ask for the money. Though infuriated and embarrassed with the entire calamity, I chalked my failure up to knowing the john personally and I set about scouting an anonymous payee at the park.

The next Sunday came and Beau and I went to the park where I was determined to begin my new career with only "no-names." Just as I assumed, a rich old gentleman approached and asked if I would like to "keep company" with him for a while. I said yes, but only if I could bring my puppy with me. He agreed. We walked to his limo where his driver, who knew exactly what was going on, opened the door for us. The smirk on that chauffeur's face made me feel dirtier than I'd ever felt (and that's saying something!). But nothing was going to stop me. I just knew I was destined to be a high-class hooker.

The limo pulled up in front of a luxurious condo and Beau and I were escorted inside and left alone with Mr. Wrinkles. I accepted his offer of a cocktail and then the three of sat on the couch (the fabric of which I'm sure cost more per yard than my monthly rent) and began talking. I was jittery, unfocused, and nervous. My brain was pulsating against the inside of my skull. I felt like my blood was trying to vault out of my body. One thing led to another and he put his age-spotted hand on my upper thigh. That's when I started sobbing.

I told him I didn't think I could continue, that I was sorry, and that I would just take my puppy and leave. He took a satin handkerchief out of his jacket pocket and kindly wiped the tears from my mascara-streaked face. He softly told me to hush, handed me a fifty-dollar bill, called for his driver and instructed him to take me home, and then the lustful but kind old man told me to keep his handkerchief.

I was surprised and confused that I'd acted in such a manner. I was mad at myself at first. I had tried it the week before and gotten the same internal reaction. My head said one thing and my heart the complete opposite. *How come Deidra can do this and I can't? What had stopped me?* I really had intended to have sex for money. I figured it would be easy money. With everything else I'd done in the past, I thought it would be a cinch. Man, was my thinking displaced! I was so inner-hollow that I didn't think I had anything else to lose or leave behind. With comparatively little harm done, I'd quickly learned that the life of a hooker is miles away from being easy money. I listened to my heart and vowed never to try this again, and I thanked God for sending me a gentleman, and for the hanky, but most of all for the ride home, sir.

THERE'S A BUTTERFLY IN THERE SOMEWHERE

1983—twenty-two years old. After a year in Phoenix working in a terribly boring job with cruddy pay, no car (it died), no friends, not being able to sell myself for money, and having to face my lecherous boss who'd already had much more of me than I could stand, I wanted to move away. That's not exactly true…What I wanted was to fall off the planet. Gravity, however, was working against me — or for me, depending on how you look at it. I called Mom and Dad and asked them if I could make a return engagement back home. They said yes, but Dad said no puppy. I had to get rid of Beau. I asked a few people if they wanted him, but didn't make that much of an effort. When I couldn't find a home, I got really high, took him to the pound, and cried for days. Once again, it seemed as if when I had finally done right by a living thing, I reverted to my usual schlocky behavior and undid all the good I had done. I did call the pound a few days later and was relieved and happy to learn that he'd gone to a good home.

After months of not talking to her, I called Deidra to tell her I was moving back to Tucson and asked if she could pick me up in Phoenix and drop me off at my parents' house. She made some obnoxious remark about not being able to make it on my own, but I chose to ignore it.

Although I had a roof over my head, being without a car at my parents' house in Tucson was definitely like being stranded in the desert (no metro transit system had yet been implemented in that part of the world). I was unproductive and self-destructive. I didn't do much of anything from sunup to sundown except drugs and go to video arcades during the day to play my new obsession — PacMan. Deidra would call and ask me to go out with her, telling me she'd pay my way. However, I didn't want to be around her. My relationship with her was changing and I was beginning to see her true character. I was frightened that I was becoming her.

I continued to numb my brain with pot, uppers, and quaaludes so I wouldn't have to think or feel. At one point, I pried the gold charms off my mother's antique bracelet intending to pawn them for drug money because I was so broke. But for some reason, when I took the last one off, I fastened them back on. Unfortunately, I ignored that same voice in my soul when it came to the ring that belonged to Buffy.

Buffy and I had been friends since the fifth grade. Although we had grown apart and barely saw each other anymore, the last time we hooked up she'd let me wear a small gold band that had been in her family for years. I sold it, thinking she would never remember my having it, but she did. When she called for it, I threw out a mirage of how I lost it, but she knew. She could still tell when I lied. Knowing I sold anything I could get my hands on, she went to the pawnshop and learned what I had done. This thread in her family's history had already been melted down. Buffy confronted me and our friendship was over. At that time, I was so morally twisted that I wasn't angry at myself for stealing from a friend, but embarrassed for being *caught*.

I also stole money from Dad. Not currency, but rolls and rolls of pennies. Dad had a thing for pennies and kept them in the den, already rolled and sorted in boxes. He had a couple of hundred bucks in rolled pennies. What I wasn't aware of was that these coins were uncirculated and in mint condition and that he was collecting them because they would be worth a lot more in the future. Every day, I took a few rolls to turn them in for quarters to play PacMan and to buy cigarettes. I intended to replenish the collection after I got a job and before he knew the rolls were missing.

Dad was doing volunteer work for the Multiple Sclerosis Society in those days, and he told me about a position opening in the main office. I interviewed and got it. I don't remember what my job description was, but I do remember being lousy at it. I didn't last there more than a month. Before I left though, I bought a car for $400 that had been donated to the chapter because it had been stuck in a flash flood in a riverbed. Believe me, a flood was the best thing for that malfunctioning piece of tin. I literally had to reassemble the inside of the car before I could drive the thing. In order to suction the sand and mud out of the cracks and crevices, the console and bucket seats had been removed and placed in the trunk. The radio was rusted, the speedometer broken, and I couldn't get the dirt and sagebrush out of the headlights, which made night driving difficult through a sand-filtered light. It matched perfectly with the haze in my head.

I had been living in the house for about two months when Mom and Dad met me in the foyer one night. Mom was crying and Dad was explosive. He'd just discovered that his daughter was stealing from him. He ordered me out of his house and though Mom knew I deserved it, she screamed at him to allow me to stay. I said I had nowhere to go but he shouted that I should have thought of that before I stole from my own father. He was right, of course. I knew I couldn't rationalize my behavior or squirm myself out this mess I had made.

I grabbed some clothes and at two o'clock in the morning, I sputtled away in my gritty car. I couldn't call Buffy, I couldn't call Sharon, and I refused to call Deidra. I had no other friends. Through stealing or lying, I had screwed over all of the other companions with whom I used to hang out and who used to let me stay at their pads. I slept for a week, alternating between my car and a park bench near downtown Tucson until I met a guy at a convenience store who let me crash at his apartment for a few weeks. I seriously contemplated suicide. I thought, *What's the use? My life is bad. I'm bad. I want to die.* Getting enough quaaludes to slumber forever was as close as a phone call. In fact, I went to a phone booth and even picked up the receiver. What stopped me were the flashes of Mom in my mind. How could I kill the spirit of the only person on Earth who expressed joy from having me around? Even with all that I had done and the umpteen times I had wrenched her heart, she was still with me, believed in me, and prayed for me to get over this part of my life and be *something*. And not just something—something *special*.

I now understand that it's hard to know when to stop pushing kids for fear they'll revolt and wind up worse than before. We must remember to talk to our kids, our nieces and nephews, our neighbors, and not be timid. Even if it seems our words are falling on deaf ears, they *are* being heard. Through all the chaos, I heard these messages and carried them with me. Those words seep into the brain, take root, and grow. And though they may not be in the forefront, they're floating around in there somewhere, ready to burn neon bright as soon as the switch turns on. Chances are, if the kid is troubled, she will make it through as long as she knows in her heart that she's truly loved. If it weren't for Mom and some other loving adults in my life like Mrs. Jaccaud, I might not be living proof.

With a Little Help From My Friend

Being kicked out of the house and losing Buffy's friendship were two of the worst things that had happened in my life. At the same time, however, they were two of the best things that could have happened to me. It's said that a person sometimes has to "bottom out" before she can help herself and start to crawl out of the quagmire of turmoil she's made of her life. Although I wasn't consciously aware of all of it at that moment, I had hit the bottom of my life. I only started to emerge and evolve when I met Wendy. She had just lost a roommate and I had just lost a home. The karmic forces at work!

Wendy was fun and cocky, and the two of us got along like bobby and pin. She didn't steal, she didn't lie, and she didn't cheat; but make no mistake, this chicklette wore no halo. Wendy was small in stature but big in mouth, with an impish grin and the raspy voice of an eighty-year-old woman who'd smoked all her life. She showed the wear and tear of early hard living and, man, could she down martinis, vodka and cranberry juice (she claimed the juice was good for a faulty kidney), and Dewar's and sodas—all as if Moses had told her they were being banned from the entire Earth the following day.

And did she love sex. When Wendy stepped out for the evening, she'd wear cute little girlie clothes, but underneath she packed a punch with a French maid corset, seamed stockings, and garter belt. You would never want to be an enemy of Wendy; but if she befriended you, she would stop at nothing to help you. Wendy was a good ol' gal with more loyalty than the Queen's guardsmen and she shared everything she had with me. She was genuine and generous and taught me how to be a friend again. Her ornery, intuitive street-smarts and don't-mess-with-me-or-my-friends attitude gave me a sense of security.

Wendy helped me break free from Deidra's clutch. She stood next to me with crossed arms, leery eyes, and a square-to-the-ground body when Deidra and I had our exchange of one another's clothes, records and jewelry in a parking lot. Even Deidra remarked about my "bodyguard," but I didn't

care. I didn't have to look over my shoulder with my
new friend.

Wendy was a few years older than I and no stranger to
life's pain and, because of her own experiences, she didn't
judge people. Wendy had a child when she was in her early
teens and her brother adopted the baby. She told me she'd
moved to Tucson at the age of twenty-five to meet her biologi-
cal parents. I'm foggy as to how that whole thing came about,
but they wound up with a hugging good relationship. Wendy
thought nothing of letting go of rubbish in her past and moving on without looking back or second guessing. She was so
good to me and gave me hope for myself.

Although I had new hope, I still had major theft problems.
I had been working at the gift shop in a motel for two months
when I was fired for stealing jewelry, candy bars, and toi-
letries. I decided to return to the restaurant business and
became a cocktail waitress in the lounge of a prominent hotel
where they trained me to tend bar. Wendy eventually came to
work there, too. I had been employed for three months and
Wendy for about half that time when, together, we were sent
packing. I had called in to get my schedule and Molly, the
manager, fired me over the telephone and then told me to tell
Wendy that she was fired, too. I thought I had job security
because I was sleeping with the owner's lawyer and found pot
for the both of them to buy. But they caught on that I had
built my bar at home with their liquor and had stolen a three-
foot, double-headed bubble gum machine out of the employee
lounge. My seedy ties with the owner probably kept them from
prosecuting me and though Wendy was aware of my sticky
fingers, she had no part of the stealing. She was terminated
through association.

Wendy wasn't upset about losing this job because she had another at a sports bar where she could work full-time. I regrouped and, within a day or two, landed another bartending position. I only worked this job for five nights. It seems Deidra knew the owner of the joint and when she found out I worked there, she called him and I was let go. I had suspected that might happen, but I rationalized that I would have never fit in that place anyway. The male clientele was all polyester, gabardine, and angel flight pants, wore multiple gold chains, and had shiny, greased-back hair. They looked like slimy gigolos and double-dealing used car salesmen. Waitresses were tall and emaciated *Hustler* magazine rejects with globs of makeup, huge bleached manes, and snooty, condescending attitudes.

Within a week, I became a singing cocktail waitress at a piano and oyster bar. I made a conscious effort not to steal from there, and didn't. I just slept with the owner once or twice under the piano after closing time (which was almost as bad as having to shuck oysters between songs). I worked with an odd-looking, switch-hitting couple. The guy looked like a fun house mirror image of Jerry Lewis, and the tone-deaf woman fashioned herself to be a Liza Minelli. Although they sometimes made me uncomfortable by trying to get me into bed with them, they were funny and made me laugh. Everyone liked me, the oysters were good, and although I was terrified to do so, I got to sing and remembered how much it was a part of me.

In the meantime, Wendy had been dating a guy from New York who frequently came into town on business. He told her he wanted to whisk her away to New York with him. In the event that something might come between their togetherness, she didn't want to find herself alone in that huge city, so she told him he had to take me, too. Fine with me. He claimed he got us airline tickets and a kitty carrier for my new kitty. Wendy put in her notice at the bar where she worked and I did the same at the mollusk sing-a-long hall. We packed our stuff, gave up our apartment, and the day before we were supposed to leave…he bolted. The schmuck was married.

But we had decided we were going to move somewhere anyway. I knew I had to leave. I was fed up with myself and detested my theft problems. Tucson was getting smaller and smaller for me. I wanted to start a new life somewhere else where nobody knew my name. Some place where I could start clean. A place where I didn't have a past. A place with no Deidra.

What's in Cincinnati Besides WKRP?

At twenty-three years of age in late October 1984, Wendy and I crammed my new used Chevette with only the barest of necessities—pots, pans, albums, clothes, bong, glass piggy bank, pillows, and my black cat creatively named Kitty.

First stop for us nomads was Mom's work to say goodbye. We were both frightened for me. I was sad to think of being without her. Though I had steered away from her in the last few years, I knew she was always within reach and here I was now with no idea when I'd see her hope-filled face again. Wendy and I didn't know where we were heading, so I couldn't even give Mom an address so she could send her first "care package." Leaving her with an "I'll call you when I get somewhere" gave us both apple-sized lumps in our throats. I chose not to say goodbye to my father. Things were so tense between us, I felt it best if he didn't see me for a while. I hoped time would perhaps numb some of the sting.

Then we drove to see Wendy's family ʳ goodbye. Same drama, just a different dauᵦ we got back in the car with tear-puffed faces, Wᵉ. me, "Well, which way? North, south, east, or west?"

Headed there from the get-go, we decided to plant our neʷ roots in New York City. Wendy, Kitty, and I quietly merged onto I-10 East.

We drove for twenty-four hours straight and I was behind the wheel somewhere around Wichita when I dozed off. Something inside my head screamed at me to wake up. This was my first profound experience that there's something larger out there. We were traveling at least sixty miles an hour and headed bull's-eye straight toward a barrier with a sign exclaiming roadwork with a large drop-off behind it. I swerved and missed it by a few feet. I wondered who or what had yelled at me. I was totally bewildered but energized. It was without a doubt a voice, but it couldn't have been Wendy, for she was sound asleep. My deceased grandmother? Guardian angel? Before this occurrence, I'd never really even given thought to those things, but this happening made me realize a divine force of some sort was on my side. When I explained to Wendy what had happened, we both took it as a sign that we were supposed to be on this adventure. We felt confident about our choice. The airline tickets to the Big Apple weren't meant to be. For some reason, however, this was.

One of our few planned stopping points was in Cincinnati. Wendy had family and friends there where we could crash and refuel for a few days.

We approached Cincinnati on what was still Halloween evening about 1:00 A.M. and could see the city's skyline from

South. I had a mystical feeling of new beginnings, oppor-
nities, and a sense of being home. Again, I was energized. I
elt like Dorothy waking up in the comfort of her own bed
after the tornado. My whole body tingled as though I were
being lifted out of my skin. I had no explanations to back up
my feelings, but I *knew* my life was headed in the right direction. As I gazed upon the lights of the Queen City in my
enlightened trance, the car started making strange sounds and
having small, shaking seizures. We had barely coasted off the
exit ramp before the car died. But what incredible luck! We
rolled to a stop directly in front of a bar! I always knew the
Jews were the chosen people!

Wendy and I left Kitty in the car and went in to have a
cocktail. We discussed the fact that we had no money to fix the
jalopy and we'd probably have to postpone our move to New
York. It didn't matter. It *felt* right with me. I had no checkbook
and no credit card, but I did have a twenty-dollar bill and a
glass pig full of pennies in the back seat of the car. (I want to
add that these pennies were not stolen from Dad, but were my
savings from several months of serving.) Wendy was not much
wealthier than I was. Although she had forty bucks in cash,
she had no checkbook, no credit card, and she had
no pig.

Wendy called Laura, a friend of hers who lived in
Cincinnati. Laura insisted that the three of us (Kitty included)
stay with her in her apartment. It was too much fun. And after
just a few days at Laura's non-stop party palace, we decided to
find jobs, forget about fixing the car, and stay in Cincinnati for
a while. I called my most wonderful Momma and told her I
wanted to try the Cincinnati spotlight on for size.

"Cincinnati!" Mom exclaimed, "What's in Cincinnati besides WKRP?"

The beginning of my new life, Mom. The beginning of my new life.

I can *feel* it.

The Rehearsal

THE COCOON IS BUSTIN'
OUT ALL OVER

My car was supposed to die in Cincinnati. I *felt* it coming over the hill on I-75, even though Cincy was to be a mere layover before wrestling New York. I listened to my gut on this one at a time when I was only beginning to acknowledge my intuitiveness and heed to the messages given from the Universe. I was meant to be in Cincinnati.

A bridge stretching over the Ohio River was the only thing that separated downtown Cincinnati from the town of Newport, Kentucky, where Laura's pad was. The Newport Yacht & Tennis Club Apartments where she lived were situated nearly at the base of the bridge. Don't let the name of the complex fool you. I know it sounds absolutely chi-chi, but the place was definitely not-not. These were regular square-roomed apartments with cheap shag carpeting and small galley kitchens. But what the heck, it would soon become home to me. After a very happy and long weekend with Laura and Wendy, it was time for me to search for a job. My car was on its last wheel, but it started up long enough for me to drive downtown and park and put in applications at every restaurant and bar that my feet passed.

Job hunting on Monday morning was the first time I'd seen daylight in several days. (Well, not really—I had seen it break a few times before going to sleep.) I fell in love with downtown Cincinnati during my first excursion. The art deco architecture, the tall buildings, and the cobblestone alleys enchanted my senses. I loved the huge brass clocks and majestic bronze sculptures and lanterns that dangled from the ornate buildings. It had been a long time since I had been around the true workmanship of the hand-carved limestone cherubs, columns, gargoyles, and figurines that graced skyscrapers. Someone from New York or Chicago might snicker at what I refer to as skyscrapers, but Tucson had only four buildings that the people there called "skyscrapers" and take it from me, none of them left even a mark on the sky. I chuckled when I knew that I must have looked like a fish out of the desert as I ran my hand over a good chunk of lapis lazuli affixed into a metal mural on the side of the Bell Telephone building at Elm and 7th Streets. The ultimate tourist, I couldn't help myself! I kept wondering how people could walk past and not look at the art that was on all corners and in between. On reflection, I doubted whether I'd ever done the same with the cactus and mountains back at the ranch.

It was the first week of November and, after living in Arizona for fourteen years, I suddenly realized that I had forgotten about the change of seasons. (Cactus thorns don't turn beautiful shades of fiery orange, red, or yellow in the fall and then glide through the air before landing on the hard, dry desert floor.) I realized, too, that all of downtown Cincinnati could fit inside Manhattan a hundred times. Nonetheless, it was plenty big for me. If we'd made it to New York, I probably would have been smushed into the cracks of the sidewalks like a smoldering cigarette. But not here. I knew instinctively that I would thrive in this town. It felt so natural to feel good! The Elm Street Café hired me as a lunch waitress and asked me to come back the next morning in the common black-and-whites (black pants, white shirt) to train. It may not have been the ideal place (whatever that is), but at least I'd soon have some cash in my pocket. Kitty and I had less than five bucks to our names and were looking to the glass pig for our financial deliverance.

Within two weeks of my start at The Elm Street Café, I received a call from Jeff Thomas, the manager of a restaurant named Rusconi's where I had put in an application. He told me this restaurant/bar was mostly gay and asked me if I was still interested to interview for a full-time job tending bar at night. I wondered why he even mentioned that. What's the difference? Of course, I wanted to come in for an interview! "I'm tickled pink," I replied. I got the job and put in my two-week notice at The Elm.

Meanwhile, Wendy, Kitty, and I moved out of Laura's apartment within a month and got a place of our own in the same complex. After I was hired, Jeff told me that the day before I submitted my application that he and the owner had had a meeting to discuss the type of personality they wanted for the bar. They'd settled on a loud, big-busted woman. Twenty-four hours later, I appeared! The Universe set this up for me knowing it would salvage me.

Rusconi's was a predominantly gay bar and I was thrilled with that. I never felt connected with a lot of the straight folks I knew and I despised that competition crap that emerged with some girlfriends. Around gays, I didn't feel like a person on the outside looking in. I was in. I was accepted as I had not been by many other groups. They liked all my fluff. In school, I never fit into a category of jock, cheerleader, or nerd. And though I entertained fellow students, especially when they egged me on in outrageous stunts, I wasn't accepted by them. When their laughter subsided, so did their need for me. With gays, I had my own category, my own label. *Me!*

The gays I'd met in the theatre, the nightclubs, and the restaurant biz, plus the few gays who were "out" in high school all liked me for me. With them, I never had to perform or prove myself. I didn't feel pressured and with them, I was relaxed and felt immediately befriended. No hoops of fire to jump through. Why is that? I think it was because I was more myself because sex had nothing to do with it. I could revel in the comfort of knowing I didn't have to give anything away, or wear a mask, or put on a flame resistant tutu to be liked. Also, maybe I was liked because gays appreciate those who hear their own rhythm. Non-conformists. They are what they are, it's a part of them. There's no choice in the matter—just as I had no choice in who I was. God knows in this homophobic society in which we live, most gay people not only have to walk to their own rhythm, but they must also make their own instruments. I never could understand all the hoopla about same sex couples. It no doubt all began with the beautifully simple explanation Mom gave me about Uncle Robert when I was a child. It never mattered to me who anyone sleeps with. Love is love.

THE CORE

This story is written for three men who added many smiles to my face: Bob "Bob-o" Brandenberg who died in 1992, Joe Wilson who died in 1993, and Chuck Pettit who died in 1995. These loving men died of AIDS-related complications.

How the Universe found for me this tiny crevice, this perfect little piece of the planet, I'll never know. What a place! Rusconi's was the prescription for whatever ailed me. Employees could wear whatever they wished and it was absent of corporate managers breathing down my neck. Many restaurants ban employees from being on the premises other than to work, but we were welcome to come in and spend our tip money at Rusconi's. We employees were not just time cards, we were members of a family, a *community* that was ever-accepting, ever-changing, and always expanding. Although we were all so different from one another, none of us was frightened or uncomfortable to be what we were. We laughed about that fact and delighted in it. I felt as if my mind had been floating around as so many loose, non-fitting pieces. Now, however, all those particles of my existence were simultaneously summoned home in harmony.

The people at Rusconi's were like characters from an art flick. There was a large older woman whom we called "Momma" because she looked like everyone's mother. And man, she made the best soups. In her apron pocket, she carried at all times *Cincinnati Magazine's* glowing write-up about her famous potato and cheddar soup and she presented the article to every customer who walked in the door (whether they were having soup or not).

Lois was an older waitress who worked only lunches and kept her fellow servers in line with her scowl. Her pace was slow and she was crotchety, but every once in a while she'd smile and that would remind us that she still had a pulse. One of the other servers was a young, effeminate, pretty boy with a hair-color-du-jour. I can't remember his real name, but we all called him "Bubbles." He had boundless energy during his shift, but was somehow always too exhausted to do the restaurant side work duties he was assigned. Edward was a quiet intellectual with an intense look and a dry sense of humor. He didn't speak much but when he did, he was worth listening to. Rusconi's had another Edward, too. This one worked in the kitchen. Nearly every day, a different woman would come into the restaurant and ask him for milk money while holding yet another one of his babies. I don't think he knew how many he had…either women or kids.

One of the cooks, Matt, looked like a chunky, drugged-out Einstein and often strayed from the medicine that kept him level. He would speak non-stop to virtually anyone about his first homosexual experiences with straight men at truck stops. Jordan was a dishwasher with a major affinity for women's clothing. One day after cleaning out his closet, he gave me a pair of bright purple fishnet stockings that he no longer used thinking I'd enjoy wearing them. (I did.)

Then there was a waitress who named herself "Edith" who was sometimes bisexual and sometimes not. Her life was a string of errors and she was the type who wasn't happy unless she was miserable. Allan smiled constantly and no matter how much food he had sizzling on the grill, he would dance, flip his spatulas in the air, and sing like a rhythm-and-blues superstar. I don't think he could cook without singing. Loreen was a beautiful girl—a lesbian, who seemed cold but actually was just reserved. She eventually took off to New York to make it big in modeling. How I laughed when she tried to make a martini for a patron and couldn't find the martini bottle! Malcolm was an awesome cook, a Rastafarian with a cat-that-ate-the-canary grin. He wore knitted hats bigger than the Mad Hatter's and was always on the lookout for the ladies.

Lionel had starched shirts, buffed shoes, and perfectly pleated pants, and his five o'clock shadow wouldn't dare appear on his never-a-hair-out-of-place head. He was studying to be a doctor, but at night wore leather pants and disco-danced in cages. Among all these, there I was—I fit in nowhere and yet I fit in everywhere.

Rusconi's was widely known as a good restaurant, and so it brought in a lot of straight people and restaurant workers who partied there after their shifts at other establishments. The atmosphere at Rusconi's was relaxed, energetic, and fun. It was a starting place, the bulb of the plant, the place where everyone gathered. Clientele and employees were gay, straight, black, white, Asian, doctor, student, politician, sewer worker— it didn't matter. I thought it a shame that it was limited to a 125-year-old building on 6th and Race Streets in Cincinnati, Ohio. Rusconi's was the way the whole world was intended to be.

Bartending was a blast. I had definitely found my calling. In addition, I'd discovered the community I so desperately needed in order to flourish. Rusconi's lounge area was small and comfortable, making it impossible not to talk to the person you sat next to. The lounge was my stage where every night was a new show. For people's birthdays, I'd pour Bacardi 151 along the top of the bar, light it, and sing "Happy Birthday" while it burned. For my own birthdays, I'd write on the sandwich board outside the number of shopping days people had left to purchase gifts until my big day. And on that "holy day," I'd supply party hats, balloons, cake, and wear a huge button that said, "Tip me big! It's my birthday!"

I came to work to see my friends and then would hang out with them during my off hours. I was invited to parties and to people's homes for dinner for whatever holiday was next on the calendar. When customers met for cocktail hour and then went out to other restaurants for dinner, they would come back and bring me take-out (especially Chinese, my fave). And they lavished me with gifts and tips. I mean I made a ton of money…and I made it honestly! They loved me! I worked from 3:00 p.m. to 3:00 a.m., Wednesday through Saturday, with the exception of being laid off for one week when I was caught smoking a joint in the basement kitchen with two other employees. I thanked God they didn't ixnay me. For punishment, they took away my bartending shifts for a week and forced me to wash dishes. (I whined so much, however, I only had to scrub for two nights.)

After living in Cincinnati for five months, I decided I should take a quick trip back to Tucson. It was time to see my father again and besides, Nancy's son Elliott, my first and only nephew, was born the previous January and I hadn't met my blood yet. I made the trip in April 1985, almost missing my plane because of all the metal I tried carrying through security. Pennies. I'd rolled fifty bucks in pennies to bring to Dad. When I got home, I laid them out on his bed. He never said a word. That's fine. He knew I was attempting to right the bad I had done.

I was twenty-four years old and finally getting my act together. I was finding me, and digging what I dug up. Stealing was no longer a part of me. I still smoked weed and nipped the grape, but hard drugs were in my past. I didn't want to numb my brain anymore, I wanted to feel it. I was also discovering an inner voice and beginning to realize that life was not just a series of unrelated events and coincidences. There's a plan. There's a plan for all of us. Astrology started to be one of my interests. And I began to meditate and to listen to my dreams. I even taught myself how to interpret them. Later, when Mom came out to visit me for the first time, she was radiant with my happiness, and all my friends loved her. For the first time in a long, long time, she was joyful for my life. She told me that Cincinnati felt like home to her, too.

It's almost as if Cincinnati possessed a vortex of energy that pulled me back and reintroduced me to people I'd known before, perhaps in a past life. I'd *sensed* I was coming home as my car sputtered around the bend on I-75 when arriving in Cincinnati, so why not believe that I was rejoining some new/old family? There was no period of adjustment or getting in tune or proving the good intentions of our friendship…we slid perfectly into one another's lives.

I met some of this world's finest inhabitants at Rusconi's. In fact, most of my present friends and business contacts are stems from Rusconi's roots. I met Rob Dorgan, Steve Bolia, David Wilson, and Greg who are my closest friends today. Even if our lives drift us apart, our souls keep us close.

INDIVIDUALLY THE SAME

Rob and Steve. Say these two names anywhere in Cincinnati and everyone knows exactly who they are. In this sleepy Midwest town of conformists and blinder-wearing folks, Rob and Steve have opened many minds while spreading their message of acceptance, love, and tolerance. They are the seeds of these biblical-basic forgotten qualities.

When I met them at Rusconi's, they didn't know each other, but they were about to become acquainted. Steve lived in an apartment (with his kitty Lefty) above the restaurant and was a customer—a curious customer. He was the manager at an elegant restaurant in a high profile hotel and engaged to be married. He somehow knew, however, that getting married wasn't the right thing to do. So why was he engaged? Because he was succumbing to the very powerful and persuasive social pressures and was trying to do what he thought his family expected of him. But something within him convinced him otherwise and he broke off the engagement, even though he wasn't certain what he wanted.

Prior to moving downtown, Steve had never met a gay person. When he sat at my bar smiling and laughing, I knew he was wearing a mask. I could sense the heaviness of his heart because he wasn't listening to it. He didn't know how to...yet. Then in walked Rob. Being an actor, Rob's timing was always perfect.

He had been going to Thomas More College to study law, but then decided the legal rat race wasn't for him. He landed a job working as a flight attendant and also waited tables at Rusconi's for extra bucks. In a few months' time, Rob, Steve, and I were patches sewn tightly together in the same quilt.

Rob was out regarding his homosexuality but like Steve, he was hiding from his soul. Rob's father had abandoned his family when Rob was a child. During his adult life, Rob had had several relationships and many a tryst, but felt that if he committed himself to one person he would eventually be forsaken.

Despite these obstacles, Rob and Steve found a complete and total love in each other—the kind that presents itself to very few people. I've watched them grow, sometimes in unison, sometimes not; but they always inspire each other's dreams and share each other's pain. They don't say things they don't mean. Respect for *themselves* as *individuals* and as a *couple* has been the footing for their thriving relationship. Their relationship has taught many (myself included) that with honesty, compassion, forgiveness, communication, and growth, love can scale obstacles and overcome impeding fears.

After fifteen years, they are so united and yet still individuals. I see the delight for one another in their faces. It's as if they had just discovered one another and are still in the six-month new-dating stage. However, they are secure and sound, taking nothing for granted, realizing the Universe can change anything at any time. Their love is absolute. These two boys are the essence of my soul.

NEVER TAKE YOUR TEETH OUT IN FRONT OF PEOPLE YOU'VE PISSED OFF!

Ralph was a weekend warrior. Monday through Friday, he worked diligently at his high-paying position at Procter & Gamble (what we Cincinnatians call Procter & God). But from Friday happy hour through Sunday twilight (including holidays), Ralph was a loud, incoherent, slobbering drunk.

Late one Saturday evening, Ralph slimed into Rusconi's and forced his cantankerous, stanky self through a herd of people. With his eyeglasses crooked and cheeks crimson, he imitated standing by pressing his lower body against the front of the bar and placing his hands flat on top for stability. His balding head with three strands of hair (all of which were out of place) hung suspended between his collapsible shoulders as if he had no neck. I could tell he was fixing to say something because his mouth was moving thick and slowly, like a dog licking peanut butter off its lips. In an impaired language that I presumed to be English, Ralph demanded a drink. I told him he was too drunk and offered him soda or coffee instead, but he would have no part in my concerned hostess-ness. He slammed a clenched fist on the bar and shouted,

"Listen, you *fat*, Nazi storm-trooper bitch! Gimme a drink!"

Fat? Did he call me fat? I couldn't care less about the other descriptives he barked…but *FAT*??? That "F'" word was the only thing I heard gush out of his loopy mouth. I couldn't believe he'd called me fat! I ordered him out of the bar.

Rusconi's manager allowed me to 86 Ralph from sitting at the bar. (When you 86 a customer, it means they're never allowed back in as long as they're breathing.) I couldn't prevent Ralph from coming into the restaurant, however. I guess Rusconi's was losing enough revenue minus Ralph's alcohol consumption that it had to be made up somehow.

Weeks after Ralph's pummeling insults, he stumbled into the restaurant and slouched drunkenly in a booth. After ordering his food, he took out his choppers, laid them on the table, put his head down, and proceeded to catnap. His table was only yards away from the bar and I stood staring him an evil eye. *Fat!* That fermented louse called me fat! He deserved something massively painful. If I'd had a handlebar mustache, I would have been twirling it between my fingers. I felt that dastardly. Onlookers, sensing slaughter, watched me stride right up to Ralph's table with my head held high. I was a soldier on a mission. I approached the sleeping dog's table and dumped several hefty splats of Tabasco sauce on the white carrots that Ralph had dangled in front of my foxy senses.

I couldn't wait until the server woke him up to eat his chow...and wouldn't you know it, he'd even ordered a Mexican omelet for the festivities. All we needed was a mariachi band! For me (and the rest of the audience), his food couldn't get there fast enough.

All eyes were on Ralph as we watched him slothfully lift his face from a pool of drool and clumsily shuffle his fingers around for his pearly whites. I held my breath while he unsuccessfully targeted his mouth with his acrylic gums. I almost shoved them in for him! But finally...a direct hit! The only sound was the steady thump of heartbeats. Not even the coffee machine gurgled. I was already feeling a rush of victory when, in a flash, Ralph's teeth hydroplaned across a wait station, a soda fountain, and three cheesecakes.

Olé!

ANYTHING CAN HAPPEN

Because Rusconi's sat across the street from one of the larger downtown hotels, many a conventioneer would wander in aimlessly. I got such a kick when the Baptist convention was in town. Ministers and male members would nearly crawl through the back door that led directly into the bar. They'd throw crumpled money on the bar, hastily order a whiskey, drink it down in one gulp, pull the brim of their hats down over their eyes, and then leave without fully standing up. It was as though they somehow believed that by not standing fully erect, they hadn't really had a toddy in a saloon.

Other conventioneers, who were not as composed, would sometimes settle on a barstool, look around, and start the name calling: faggot, dike, homo, and the like. I would always tell them that this was our home and that they were welcome to stay, so long as they shut up. Sometimes they cooled down, sometimes not. I became one of the people coworkers counted on to ask people to leave the premises if things got out of hand. It was one of my favorite things to do.

In one encounter, a Shriner staggered into the bar. He was wearing a tasseled hat and a sash loaded with medals and ribbons, so I figured he must have been a good scout. After ordering a scotch, he peeked at his surroundings and began spewing obscenities. I almost called the cops to have him removed because he wouldn't pipe down, but I decided this was a job for Gator, a bearded, tattooed, whale-girth of a man who drove a cab. I told the Shriner that this joint obviously was not for him but that I knew where he would thoroughly enjoy his manly self. He seemed relieved that I was hip to his fancies, so I called Gator, gave him ten bucks, and told him to drop this expert specimen of stupidity off at The Dock and then drive away fast. The Dock was a big, gay, cha-cha palace just south of downtown, and they specialized in drag shows on that particular night of the week. I only wished I could have seen the Shriner's face.

I learned to never acknowledge a customer outside of the restaurant unless he acknowledged me first. Most homosexuals and lesbians were not openly gay in right-wing cities like Cincinnati during those years. Many of Rusconi's gay clientele were teachers, police officers, doctors, politicians, and executives from Cincinnati's Fortune 500 corporations. They were justifiably fearful of losing their jobs if they were known to be gay. This practice of aware-unawareness was also granted to the straight couples who were having extramarital affairs, because they'd secretly meet at Rusconi's thinking they'd be safe in a gay bar.

On one Halloween eve while Mom was visiting, an angry husband waited outside with a baseball bat to clobber his wife's paramour as the two left the bar. Mom and I were cleaning up, not knowing what was about to transpire, when in ran the wounded lover, holding his noggin and screaming like a banshee with blood gushing out of his head. Mom exclaimed, "Wow! Look at his costume! It looks so real!"

THE HOST

The Conservatory was the biggest, baddest, meat market disco in all of Northern Kentucky. Wendy and Laura were cocktail waitresses there and although I wasn't part of the staff, I was part of the Conservatory "family." It was in the game room playing PacMan that I met a man twelve years my senior and with whom I subsequently had a one-night stand that lasted three years. He was my first "real" boyfriend and his name was Tim.

The relationship, if you can call it that (he mostly had a relationship with himself), started out in a game room, and for him, it stayed in a game room. We had gone out on four or five dates before he remembered that he was married and had a child. He and his wife were, *of course*, headed for Splitsville. I should have run in the opposite direction as fast as I could, but I didn't. I desperately wanted a relationship. It didn't matter that Tim and his wife were still living together. Actually, it didn't really matter all that much *who* wanted me. I just wanted to be wanted.

I got pregnant during the first few months of the relationship. After my gynecologist discussed several alternatives with me, I didn't see any other option but abortion. Before I left her office, she called to make an appointment for me at a woman's clinic to begin the initial proceedings. I was told there was a follow-up visit and then a one-week "cooling off" period after that, to make sure my decision was well thought out and final. I took it very personally that some people assumed I thought nothing of this action I was about to take—like I believed it was as morally easy as getting a mole removed. I believe passionately that people do have the right to choose what they want for their body. I found it repugnant that some would consider me a murderer.

Tim was out of town on a business trip, so I called him on the phone and told him I was pregnant. He didn't think there was any way he could be responsible and he questioned me as though I were a criminal. This man I was nuts about and faithful to didn't think enough of me to take me for my word. On the other hand, I didn't think enough of me to walk away from him. Neither Tim nor I wanted the child. I had no intention of bartending my way through full term and then being a mother at twenty-four years of age. In fact, I didn't think I'd ever want kids. But even with this knowledge, making the decision to have an abortion was frightening, soul-violating, and cheapening.

As soon as I got off the phone with Tim, I was immobilized, appalled that my boyfriend was so insensitive. The phone rang again and I hoped it was him calling to apologize. It wasn't. It was Mom. I hadn't planned on telling her—why worry her 1,800 miles away?—but after making light chatter for two minutes, she asked me flat out, "Carol, are you pregnant?" I broke into tears and kept asking her how the hell she knew. All she could say between tears was, "I had a feeling. I just had a *feeling.*"

Tim and I finally decided we would go fifty-fifty on the cost of the abortion. That, however was the extent of his participation in the trauma. His only concern was how *he* was going to get out of this mess. Wendy wanted to take me and pick me up from the clinic so I wouldn't have to drive. She even offered to stay in the waiting room so I wouldn't be alone, but I wanted Tim to do something for me. I asked him to be my transportation and he obliged, but only reluctantly. The clinic accepted only cash or money order for the procedure, so that morning he stopped at a convenience store for me to buy a money order.

I'll never forget that moment. There I was, going into a place where people usually purchased gum, soft drinks, and gas, and I was there to buy a "ticket" for an abortion. Without the support of my boyfriend, I felt so uncared for, disposable, disgraced, and full of shame. I tried to keep quiet and not utter a word so Tim wouldn't be mad. I felt like I was a naughty child being scolded by my father. But when I slumped back into the car, I could no longer hold back the tears, which he proceeded to ignore. I kept thinking that if he would just look at me, *really* look at me, he would feel something other than anger about what was going on. All I wanted was a soft word or to have my hand held. It's obvious to me now that I gave him way too much credit. He was incapable of feeling.

Tim left me at the clinic with no smile, kiss, or semblance of encouragement. I guess I should have been happy that he came to a complete stop before I got out of the car. Afterwards, he was three hours late in picking me up and I had to sit in the waiting room and watch the next herd of abortioners carry out their sorrowful requests. I had no cash to call a cab and I couldn't endure a bus ride. I could have called one of my many friends, but I didn't want anyone to know how badly my boyfriend had mistreated me. When he finally showed up, I asked him how he could have left me sitting and waiting. "I got caught up in a meeting," he snapped. "I'm a working man, you know!" Then he said nonchalantly, "So, how'd it go?" It was as though he'd asked if I'd just had coffee with some friends. "Okay," I muttered. And that was the last time it was mentioned. I didn't tell him how it went. He didn't want to hear. He didn't want to know.

A day rarely slips by that I don't think about it. However, I don't "what if?" my decision of May 1985. When I see bumper stickers reading "Choosy Mothers Choose Life" and "Abortion Stops a Beating Heart," I want to shout to the people in those cars and tell them about my dire situation, my heartache, my tears, my story. Maybe I can make them understand that it's not a simple black-and-white situation, that I'm not a cold-blooded killer, that abortion should be left up to the woman to decide and not the government or a horde of self-righteous bumper sticker owners. It was an extraordinarily difficult and painful decision, but I feel at peace knowing that I did what was best for all. (As a side note, one week before the abortion, I became sick and wound up in the hospital for one night. My doctor found cysts in my ovaries that were bursting poisons. She told me there was a high probability I would miscarry.)

Since I believe there is a reason for everything, I have searched forever for the answer to why this happened in my life. The solace to my never-ending quest is that I believe a soul needed my body for that small amount of time. That this agreement for me to be host was ordained before my birth. I was told that by a metaphysical healer six years after I had the abortion. He had no knowledge of my past and even told me the baby was a girl by the name of Sara, and that she loves me and thanks me. I froze when he said that. When I played house as little girl, I named my baby dolls Sara. I realize that I had *free will* and could have gone an alternate route. But it happened, and I believe I was supposed to do what I did.

I felt better knowing there was a reason for this to have occurred in my life but until now, I've been silent about what that healer told me in 1991. I didn't want to give the baby a name. I didn't want to think that the *thing* inside me was a tiny human. Sara…my baby…the soul who used my womb—her karma was not mine. She had her own destiny to follow, as I followed mine.

HUSH

This story is dedicated to Terry LaBolt and Michael J. Leonard who are quite dear to my heart. Terry has been surviving HIV-AIDS since 1985, and Michael since 1986.

Ron told me he had AIDS while we were crossing the street. He had been HIV positive for a year before becoming full-blown, but he didn't tell anybody. He was ashamed. Worse, his family was ashamed of him. I felt slammed in the gut. I couldn't breathe and my knees began to give out in the middle of the crosswalk. The year was 1987 and AIDS was just making its deadly and silent debut in Cincinnati. It was scarcely talked about—even at Rusconi's where everyone was accepting. And when it was, the talk was ever so soft and reluctant, as if the disease would go away if not acknowledged. I understood little of AIDS, as did Ron, but he filled me in the best he was able. He planned to tell only the few of his friends he thought could handle the jolt of what he called this very mysterious, fatal, and disreputable disease.

I had met Ron through Rusconi's. He was then about thirty, had a prematurely receding hairline, spoke with a Southern drawl that he hated, and was as tall as Lurch. I nicknamed him my "joke man" because he would sometimes write down the funnies I spat out, and laugh thunderously at each one I revealed—the nastier, the better. Ron was a waiter at a restaurant in the Westin Hotel but came to Rusconi's after work. Each night, he brought me all the fresh flowers from the tables where he worked and combined them into one huge bouquet with the stems bundled together by a wet napkin and then wrapped in tin foil. Although he wasn't much of a drinker—or a talker—he loved sitting at my bar. Ron was an observer whose eyes took in everything that was happening and whose ears picked up everyone's conversations. He could dish it out with the best of 'em, but only in fun. I never heard Ron say a bad word about anyone.

I can pinpoint the week he was diagnosed. Ron crashed while riding his racing bicycle, tore up some skin, and went to the hospital. He was released immediately after being patched up, but didn't go back to work for a while. I had spoken to him on the phone during his recuperation and found him to be aloof and more quiet than normal. When he finally showed up at Rusconi's after his first night back at work, he appeared uneasy. I remember how he stared into the glass of juice he held tightly in his hand and didn't look up or tune into anything but his own zone. I could see that he had a huge welt on his forehead and deep scratches on other parts of his body. I kept telling him that everything would be fine and that he'd be back on his bike in no time. When I reached out to hold his hand, he pulled back from me, although not immediately. He seemed to contemplate it for a moment or two. In a few seconds and with tears thick in the rims of his eyes, he reached for my hand and whispered, "I'm not going to get better." Then he left. Something was wrong. Something was very wrong.

Although he finally let me know that he was battling the disease, he still kept a distance between us. For several months, we talked on the phone, but he kept our conversations to a light chatter and he refused to let me see him. I wanted to. I wanted to hug him. I was horrified to think of how many other people might be out there who felt so alone, frightened, unloved, and ashamed. Nobody should have to live like that. Nobody should have to die like that.

Ron was unconscious and in the hospital when a small group of his close friends, me included, went to see him. Each of us had a private time with Ron. When my turn came, I sat beside his bed and held his once strong and steady hands that God had made to pump out symphonic sounds on the organ and to play classical piano. Now they were liquid. I couldn't help but stare at the purple-red lesions all over his feet and ankles. Almost all of his hair had fallen out and he had more bone weight than muscle weight. His eyes were open, but the bright blue in them had thinned into a pale gray. His breathing was so loud and erratic that every time he took a breath, I didn't think he'd have the strength to do it again. I kept telling Ron that I loved him and not to be frightened because there was a whole new world for him. I promised him that this new world wouldn't hurt.

Ron was the first person I knew—at least of whom I was aware—who died of AIDS.

I was furious. I was so damned angry and scared at the same time. I found AIDS to be big, mean, sneaky, and out of control. It was an epidemic for heaven's sakes and no one was talking about it! No one understood it. I feared that little was being done to find a cure because many thought the world would be better off without "queers" and "drug addicts." I felt powerless. I went to Ron's funeral, but I didn't have any money at that time to donate in his honor to an AIDS charity. That's what he wanted his friends to do. His family however, appeared to want no part in any of it. I promised myself that someday, when I was able, I would do more.

Ronald A. Stephens
April 5, 1955 – January 20, 1990

THE CAPERS ARE MINE!

I stayed with Tim through his petty divorce (yes, they finally did get divorced). There was much bickering between Tim and his wife and they both used their beautiful little child like a commodity against each other. When their divorce was final, Kitty and I moved out of my apartment into his house. Wendy and I parted as friends, but we didn't spend much time together after we weren't roomies. Nothing went wrong; we just went our own separate ways. You know, it's funny as you look back upon all the different phases of your life and upon all the people who are splashed throughout who meant so much to you and you could never imagine not having them by your side. Then they disappear. Or maybe it's you who disappears from their life. Perhaps she and I were supposed to meet so we could wind up in Cincinnati and after that, her cosmic errand with me was done.

But now I had other roommates to deal with: Tim, his ego, and his selective amnesia—all of which left very little room for me. I found out (from his friend, by accident), that he had married and divorced his first wife twice. In fact, months before his friend blabbered, Tim had mentioned to me in a joking manner that he had married her twice. I asked him if he was serious and he said no, he was just kidding. So when his buddy told me about Tim's twice-wife, I thought there must be something to it. Tim couldn't understand why I was angry and hurt that he had lied to me. He thought it was no big deal. He had the power (which I now know I gave him) to make me feel silly about my emotions. I wound up apologizing to him for being mad in the first place. I wasn't angry about the past, only about his dishonesty. But sometimes you want something so badly, you second-guess your own feelings and make slight of them. Through rationalizing and justification, you accept the other person's poor behavior while simultaneously ignoring *your* honor, *your* ideals, *your* self. This was the recipe of our relationship.

When I first moved in with Tim, I was so proud of the first nice piece of furniture I bought—a mahogany, Queen Anne cocktail table. He told me to put my initials under the table so when we broke up, we'd know what belonged to whom. Although he flashed his handsome salesman-smile when he said it, I remember the alarm going off inside of me. Unfortunately, when it came to Tim, I paid little attention to my inner voice.

One time at home, I dropped a drinking glass I was washing. It broke and cut my hand and bled terribly for a few minutes. Even after it stopped bleeding, I kept pressing on my wound to make it keep bleeding so when Tim came home from work, he would feel badly for me and tend to my injury. I was aware of what I was doing and angry with myself for dragging my past behavior into my present. I realized I was still the same idiot I was in the seventh grade when I'd scratch the inside of my nose until it bled and then act oblivious to it until a squeamish student would point and scream and everyone would come running. When Tim came home, and I thrust my wrapped-in-bloody-towel lacerated paw at him and all he could say was that I was a moron for not going to the emergency room.

After two years together, I told Tim, "Marry me or I'll have to go." Darned if we didn't start planning a date for our wedding a full year away. I'll never forget Mom's words when I called her to give her the news: "Carol darling, if you can take being third on his list (his child being second) for the rest of your life, then this marriage may work." I wasn't sure what she meant at that time, but I did know in my soul that the wedding would never happen.

When dear Momma flew to Cincinnati to seek out reception halls and brought her wedding dress to be fitted to my form, I knew I would never wear it walking down the aisle towards Tim. I even remember wondering why I was throwing away money on invitations. If I knew I'd never hear the music, why was I doing the dance? Because I was scared, that's why. I was scared that Tim was the only man on Earth who would be willing to marry me and I was frightened that if I didn't get married, who would take care of me? I didn't think I could make something out of myself and truly become self-sufficient. The last three months with him were horrific. It wasn't until he told me he had another woman and screamed at me to get out that I did.

The instant Tim told me to scram, my close friends Rob Dorgan and Steve Bolia called because they said they knew something was wrong. Through my disjointed gibberish, they made out that Tim had another toy and that it was time for me to move on. They had been pushing me to leave him for a couple of months and although they were sad that I was hurting, they were happy Tim and I were kaput. I followed their orders and grabbed some makeup, clothes, and my hair dryer and tossed everything in a laundry basket. Been there before, but this time I didn't sleep on a park bench—I had Rob and Steve's apartment, and was offered many other places to stay.

Mom called (she always has perfect timing) while I was in a stupor gathering articles. I told her my life was over and I'd never get over this. "No darling, your life is not over. Don't say that. It's actually just beginning. I know it doesn't seem that way right now, but this is the best thing. You'll get it together and you'll soon realize you deserve so much more from a man! Get out and take everything that's yours! Everything!"

Within a week of being dumped, I found a cool apartment downtown. All I had to do was get my things from Tim's, and so I called him and set a date. About twenty friends, all of whom I met through Rusconi's, volunteered to help me move. We gathered at Rusconi's at nine o'clock on a Sunday morning with coffee cups clenched in our hands and sleep still in our eyes—everyone except me...I hadn't slept for weeks. When I walked into the restaurant and saw all those faces who loved me and only wanted the best for me and couldn't wait for this to be behind me, I knew I would be more than okay. They hated Tim for what he had put me through and they were all there for me, holding my soul together and gently guiding me along.

The laughter started right away. I rented a thirty-six-foot truck that my friend Bill Lindenschmidt drove, followed by seven cars full of gay men. It was a major Priscilla convoy! As I bounced like a trucker in the passenger seat of the cab, I'd look back in the side mirror at the carnival of cars trailing behind and couldn't help but smile—smile and cry, smile and cry. For the twenty-minute drive, the horns trumpeted from all the cars like someone had just gotten married and they were still sounding off when we lined up in front of Tim's house in Mariemont, a conservative, Catholic neighborhood.

Ringing the doorbell to what used to be my home was a strange moment. The spiteful pig knew I was coming and answered the door as if I had awakened him, acting totally surprised to see me. He even suggested that we return in a few hours so he could get ready. Not a chance! I felt so strong with all my friends behind me and we weren't budging. Tim had had his five-year-old child (who had no clue what was happening) along with his new gal pal and her young kid there to watch the circus.

The first thing I wanted was to get Kitty. A few days before the move, I called Tim and asked him not to let her out so she wouldn't be prowling about the neighborhood, but he ignored my request. As soon as I called for her, however, she came running from behind the house. I put her in the cab of the truck and then my army and I marched into the barracks.

Being in Tim's home with all those busy queens buzzing around was like being in the midway of a fair. Randy asked me if he could do the honor of fetching my clothes and shoes from the closet because he loved my outfits. "I can't wait to get my hands on them!" he said excitedly rubbing his hands together in anticipation. My friends instructed me to do nothing but point out what was mine, while they gathered everything and took it to the truck. I pointed to the couch where my replacement was nervously smoking a cigarette. She politely moved to the floor and resumed staring at the TV. Then I pointed to the TV and the TV stand. Soon she was sitting on the floor in a barren room with a cigarette burning in the ashtray, but not for long. The ashtray belonged to me, too. (Thank heavens she wasn't wearing any of my clothes!) I took the toilet paper off the roller. It was mine...I had bought it. I wanted so badly to peel the contact paper off the kitchen shelves, but Rob and Steve wouldn't let me.

Vermont and Chuck got my dryer out of the basement and Chuck didn't even get upset when he broke a nail. I'm still mad that we didn't get the ceiling fan, but Darrell reminded me that I had more class than to leave a big hole in the ceiling for Tim's kid to stare into. But we did get the porch swing! True, I was moving to a downtown apartment where there was no porch, but Mom's voice echoed in my head *Get out and take everything that's yours! Everything!*

It was at that very moment, almost as if I were under an hypnotic spell, that I went to the refrigerator, opened the door, and grabbed the capers. After all, the capers *were* mine. He didn't even know what capers were before I moved in. And the nerve of him, asking for my engagement ring back. I had planned to sell it and keep the cash...and I did.

This nightmare in my life was humorous because of the love and friendship that engulfed me. I felt like garbage after taking all Tim's deception and selfishness and then being ousted. But with the spirited love for me of these gay men, I got through this time without turning ugly towards myself.

When One Door Closes...

Kitty and I dug our new dwelling. It was a loft apartment, all open, with no walls or doors, except one for the water closet. An entire wall of the apartment was floor-to-ceiling windows which Kitty especially enjoyed during the morning sun. I was a downtown bohemian-sophisticate now and just a few blocks from Rob, Steve, and my good friend David Wilson in the middle of bar loop and a hop and skip from work. What I loved most about my new crib were the lights of the city at night and the steady hum of traffic going over the bridges that meld downtown Cincinnati with Kentucky. It made lonely moments less wobbly.

I had a blow-out party at my new pad about a month after I moved in. It was on the date that I was supposed to marry what's-his-name: February 14, 1987. The best part about breaking up with someone is losing weight, and I could finally pour my bod into a black lace number that Mom had bought for me months before. About forty friends (all men) came over to celebrate my new life and that night I received my first knock on the door from apartment security to lower the music. The funny thing was that I didn't have a stereo yet. It was just me and the boys whoopin' it up!

Getting over my ex-fiancé wasn't difficult. I wasn't keen, however, on being single again. I missed not having a person next to me in bed. It wasn't *Tim* I missed though. I know now that it wasn't *him* that I wanted so much and was so afraid to lose. I didn't think about what was wrong with the failed relationship or why I put up with someone who treated me poorly. I didn't think about why I disappeared when in a relationship. I didn't know that I had to fill myself up to feel whole. I was depending on someone else to do it for me. All I thought about was finding my next boyfriend. And in a short time, I did.

Sean had a face like a GQ angel and when he was sober, the lines he recited waltzed beyond charming. Then the whole mistake belched into a savior complex on my part. Sean was the textbook alcoholic. I thought I could change his ways, of course, and make him walk the straight and narrow. While I thought that perhaps all he needed was a good woman, he thought all he needed was five or six bad ones. I wasn't ignorant to his lies and fooling around. I would catch him because he was drunk most of the time and couldn't remember which broad he told what to. However, I felt like Sean really needed me, whereas Tim had a take-me-or-leave-me attitude.

Then another era ended: Rusconi's. The first three years there, I had an ideal work life, but the last several months were strange times. I felt this glorious place was slowly losing life. The manager turnover became non-stop and the owners started enforcing ridiculous rules and stopped upkeep and maintenance on equipment. Long-time employees left suddenly. Paychecks bounced. The kitchen ran out of food on weekends, as the bar did of booze. Delivery guys didn't accept checks from the restaurant anymore, only cash. The ambiance changed. Management wrote me up for insubordination for the first and only time in three years. (I wasn't even written up when I was caught smoking a joint in the basement!) It was slowly becoming impossible to continue there, so I followed my fellow employees and found a cocktail position at the Lobby Lounge in the Westin Hotel.

With a heifer-sized lump in my throat, I gave my two-week notice at Rusconi's. But before that time was up, Rusconi's closed its doors. Actually the doors were closed for them. I came to work to find the restaurant wrapped up like a Hanukkah gift in yellow IRS tape. It had been closed down by the federal government for nonpayment of taxes. There was a sign on the door instructing all employees to come back at 2:00 p.m. to get their paychecks. What a dreadful day. When I returned, the owners and their lawyer were there along with government officials, all of them standing in the dark with a flashlight because the electricity was shut off. The owners didn't talk to anyone. They just stood like dead trees handing out our pay. A part of me died that day. Although for the past few months, my safe kibbutz had been a little unbalanced—it was now blown to pieces.

The Westin was polyester uniforms, signing in and out for breaks, and heavily starched managers. I didn't realize how much I despised it until Robert Jindra and David Devereaux (two customers from Rusconi's) stepped in, smiling and happy to see me and I broke down in tears. I had just been written up (I'd only been there two weeks) for eating an M&M in public view. I held onto those boys so tight, not wanting to let go. They represented the only fragment of me I could still see. At the Westin, I felt like I was back in high school. I was no one special, nobody brought me food, toys, or flowers. No one paid any attention to me, there was no one to listen to my jokes or stories, no laughter, and no one that I could mother. I was just one of the five hundred name-tagged, android employees. Inside, I was terrified that I was about to hop on the job roller coaster again.

...ANOTHER ONE OPENS

"You have so many friends," Nancy said happily, "but what you really need is a *girlfriend*. Someone you can go shopping with and do your nails with. You know, someone you can dish and giggle with. There's nothing like a best girlfriend."

Those were the last sentences of our phone conversation before I left for John and Eric's for dinner. I told my sister I have lots of friends to do nails and giggle with...they all just happen to be guys. I hadn't thought about it, but her words left a pebble in my heart. All my friends were male and I hadn't any connection with Wendy and Laura anymore.

John, Eric, and I were outside on their patio starting to eat when a car pulled into the driveway. We watched two intoxicated young women slide out of the car and weave their way toward us. The two, who happened to be John and Eric's upstairs neighbors, were so soused they were flammable. John was about to introduce us when the redheaded broad sat down on my lap and began to eat my steak and fettuccine Alfredo. When she was done cleaning my plate, she and the other walking bottle of champagne started a water fight with each other with the garden hose. There I sat, listening to the guttural yearnings of my stomach, watching two grown women hose each other down like kids running through a sprinkler in summer. Paula McQuown was the redhead and Barbara Horkey was her roommate. They soon stumbled through the front door of the building and I could still hear them giggling as their sloshing bodies tripped up the steps toward their apartment.

I was at John and Eric's not only because they invited me, but also because I was keeping busy with friends and avoiding the incessant telephone calls from my on again/off again (we were off again at the moment) boyfriend, Sean. For at least a month now, I had been seriously trying to rid myself of him. I knew I wanted and deserved better, but he gave me stuff that Tim didn't. I liked that, and so I masked all the bad with the little good. He was physically attentive, liked to cuddle, and he told me that he loved my ethnic look and that I was beautiful—constantly. I know it was superficial, but with him dripping me in compliments and the fact that he was a good lover (something else I'd never had), I kept taking his pickled butt back. Once again, I was at the mercy of my friends, so I wouldn't be swayed by Sean's suavity over the phone lines.

My friend John was not only a good cook and gracious host, he was also the manager of the Palm Court Lounge at the Omni Netherland Plaza Hotel downtown. I had given the Westin a fair try for three months and could truthfully say that

I despised it as much then as I had on the first shift. That evening, John told me that the Palm Court needed cocktail waitresses and that I should come in for an interview. He added that his soused and waterlogged neighbors were also employed there. And that's where the job roller coaster dropped me off. It wasn't too long a ride.

THE TROUBLE WITH PANTYHOSE – #2

The Omni Netherland Plaza was a frenzied place during football season. This grand hotel in downtown Cincinnati is only blocks away from the Bengal's football stadium and offered inexpensive weekend sports packages. One particular football afternoon, the Palm Court Lounge was understaffed, to say the least. I was the only cocktail waitress for ninety beer-guzzling, nacho-eating, belly-scratching hotel guests, and Paula, the red-head who sat on my lap at the dinner party she wasn't invited to, was the only bartender. She and I had become instant friends.

A colossal, corn-fed woman was hoarding all my attention as she chewed me up and spit me out because she had been waiting on a club sandwich and french fries for almost an hour. I knew she must have been famished because when her stomach growled, I swear the wall sconces flickered on and off. I understood her anguish and already had run into to the kitchen (also short on help) several times to check on it. Finally, she screamed, "The second coming of Jesus will be here before my sandwich!" At that precise moment, a kitchen guy brought her food out and placed it at the end of the bar. I guess Jesus heard her.

My eyes fixated on the plate as I rushed forward ready to

grab it up. Then a disciple of the devil appeared out of nowhere and knocked her mound o' food to the floor. I covered my ears with my hands, and with the loud meat-and-potatoes crowd grumbling faintly in the background, opened my mouth and erupted an invisible scream. Paula, up to her elbows in bottle caps and overflowing ashtrays, saw the whole scene. Our eyes met and we both laughed into the next day.

Little LuLu finally got a sandwich and I tried not to let anything break my cocktail waitressing spirit, but it was getting mighty tough. There's only so much…

"Hey, babe, fetch me another brew!"

…a refined lady such as myself can take. I wanted so very badly to reply, with one hand groped on my genitalia, "Fetch this, buddy!" But I demurred. I already had one disciplinary write-up for wearing antlers on my head while I worked on a Christmas Eve.

Professional that I was, I kept working. As I maneuvered through this toothless standing-room-only crowd and holding a tray of drinks high into the air, I tried to squeeze through two large, velvet, winged-back chairs. The chairs grabbed my wrap-around skirt and pulled it to the floor. There I was, skirtless, in the middle of the Palm Court Lounge…a plump Statue of Liberty with a tray of cocktails in place of the torch. *Welcome to America! Land of liberty, justice, and alcohol!* I remained frozen in place for a moment, quite impressed with myself for not spilling a drink. It was a scene eerily reminiscent of the Rubiyat several years earlier: nude hose and, of course, no undies. I casually lowered my tray and handed it to a woman whose husband and teenage son were staring directly at my crotch. I reached for my skirt, wrapped it around me like a towel, and scampered through the lounge and into the restaurant and through the mirrored door that led to an employee sitting room. I faintly heard the lady with my tray of drinks yelling, "What do you want me to do with this?" I had half a mind to tell her.

I got a couple of safety pins from a fellow employee, resurrected my composure, and within minutes returned to the coliseum to face the lions. Thankfully, because the lounge was so crazed, not a whole lot of people saw my X-rated impersonation of Ms. Liberty. I found the woman in the same spot I left her—holding my tray of melting, undelivered cocktails. Her husband and son…well, they were in the same spots, too, and still wearing the same dazed grins. As I thanked the woman for holding my tray, her boy, who was wearing a Future Farmers of America jacket, shouted, "We're from Peebles, Ohio!" Assuming that the closest this young kid may have come to nakedness is a farm animal—I probably looked very fine to him.

COLORADO, HERE I COME!

I couldn't imagine not being around them all the time. Worse would have been not being able to call them twelve times a day to involve them in my every crisis and breakdown. How was I going to deal with this? How was I going to survive with Rob and Steve living in the wilderness of Colorado for an entire freakin' year? I couldn't believe they were leaving me! It took them weeks to convince me not to take their leaving so personally, saying they were on a quest for spiritual growth, tranquility, and inner peace. The poor guys didn't even invite me, but they wound up with me anyway!

Colorado had called to the boys and they listened. A well-known astrologer named Linda Goodman whom they followed religiously lived in Cripple Creek, a tiny, old, broken-down mining town nestled on the western slope of Pikes Peak. Cripple Creek was to be their home. I had nothing better to do and didn't want to be without the boys. I had interests in astrology and could use a break from the daily drudge, and lord knows I hungered for inner peace.

I had been working at the Omni for over a year. Paula had moved to another hotel and it just wasn't the same without her, and I'd been thinking of looking for employment elsewhere. I had been free of Sean for months, but like a buoy in a tempestuous sea, he had recently popped up in my life again. He was in a twelve-step program now, but only after receiving an ultimatum from his employer. The program wasn't working for him—he just wouldn't drink before a meeting.

Kitty and I moved out of my cool loft apartment and shacked up with our good friend David Wilson (another former Rusconi-ite) for a couple of months to save on rent. Rob and Steve purchased a blue 1979 Jeep Wagoneer with no electric windows, no tape deck, no sun-roof, and no air conditioning. This is not how a Jewish gal should travel but since I really wanted to go, I dealt with it. Weeks before leaving, we collected small stacks of only the necessary items we needed to make our rental house a home. This is what I learned the eve of departure: a VCR and TV are NOT necessary; a salad spinner and waffle iron are NOT necessary; a shower caddy and gadget shelf are NOT necessary. I quickly discovered that every item that to me represented essential luxury and comfort was NOT necessary. Why didn't they just siphon the blood out of me so I'd take up less room?

When our small piles of stuff combined to make a huge heap, we began to realize how tiny the back of their vehicle with two cats (Steve's Lefty and my Kitty), a litter box, two men, and one whiny Jewish broad really was.

On the second evening of the journey while Rob drove and Steve napped, the blue beast ran out of gas in the middle of Missouri. We caucused and formulated a plan. Steve would stay with the Jeep and the felines, while Rob and I hitched a ride to the nearest gas station.

Off we went with a flashlight and a dented gas can. I didn't think it was safe for a Jewish liberal female and a gay man to be thumbing it in a part of the country that I judged to be just short of advertising Klan meetings on billboards. My paranoia was racing away with itself. They kill people like us out there, I reasoned. After about twenty minutes, a beat-up, rusted-out, U.S.-flag-decaled Chevy pulled over to pick us up. As we opened the door, Rob and I were taken aback by the condition of the car and the driver. The first thing I spotted was a home-fabricated rifle rack by the slanted rear window. The rack was wedged in between the sides of the car and secured tightly by bundled rags on each end. Flaked foam bulged through the rips in the fabric seats and the ceiling looked as if a cat had gotten its nasty vengeance on someone who hadn't cleaned its litter box for ages. The man was bulky, like a bouncer at a stadium rock concert. You could tell he needed more space, but the shape of the car kept him from spreading out. This grungy-darker-than-a-charcoal-briquette black man with a yellow-tooth grin (yes, tooth) invited us to hop in. We did, albeit hesitantly.

His name was Scott, and he was polite and talkative, telling us about his wife and kids and his job as a coal miner. He drove us past the exit to his work to the nearest gas station which was a good eight miles. Then he drove us back to the turn-off about three miles from our lifeless Jeep. He said he was sorry for not being able to take us all the way, but he was late for work. *He* was sorry? We should have apologized to him.

Being seasoned pros now and confident that the Universe was holding us in the palm of her hand, we stuck out our thumbs again. This time, a nearly new Ford pulled over. This car had no gun rack. A nicely dressed, young, white couple with a child greeted us and, from start to finish, preached to us about converting. They insisted we would be condemned to the fires of hell if we continued to turn our backs and refused to be saved by the Lord Jesus Christ. Now *they* kill people like us! Little did they know that by listening to them, we felt we were already in hell. In fact, if we had had to ride with them any longer we would have killed ourselves just to end our misery. Thank heavens the jaunt was a short one. If Steve, Rob, and I'd had tails, we would have seen them wag.

Steve poured the gas into old Blue's belly and we drove to a feeding station where she had her fill. And being the Virgo that he is, Steve then taught Rob and me the right way to read the gas meter so if he napped again, we wouldn't wind up in the same situation. But that day, I learned much more than how not to run out of gas.

COLORADO, THERE I GO!

I had never seen so many stars. The Colorado night sky embroidered a plush comforter of bright lights above my head and shooting stars were an every-minute miracle. This place was an open zoo: antelope, ram, deer, elk, and the fattest white rabbits you ever saw roamed freely. The breezes smelled like smooth Pine-Sol without the twang of ammonia. But even with all this nature and wholesomeness, I couldn't wait to get my used-to-pollution-cellulited-butt back to Cincinnati. I appreciate clear air and open wilderness for a vacation getaway; but to live in, I'll take the rancid odor of a city garbage truck in the sweltering summer heat over the clean and crisp any day.

Cripple Creek was not a place for a little Jewish girl with an attitude. I had more teeth in my mouth than the four hundred and seventy-four populace combined. The nearest gas station was sixty miles away in Colorado Springs. There were no 7-Elevens, Walgreens, boutiques, grocery stores...nothing. Not even a craft shop with plaster geese dressed in raincoats. When I say nothing, I mean *nothing*. Even the only laundromat was defunct. How was I going to live in a place where the only business open year-round was a taxidermist?

True, we arrived in April and "season" in Cripple Creek didn't begin until May when the gift shops and restaurants unlocked their doors. The three of us had jobs lined up as singing waiters in the Palace Hotel (a place known for hauntings), which also opened the busy month of May. In that magical month, the town opened its creaky arms to tourists wanting to wander in old gold mines and experience a few hours of the Wild West.

Rob made all the arrangements for our rental home over the phone. All I can say is that the photo the realtor had sent us had been greatly enhanced. When we crossed the threshold, we stepped over beer bottles, rusted empty food containers, and old newspapers. Did I mention that we found a deer leg in the basement? It also seems that the realtor had neglected to tell us we had to have the water and electricity turned on and get the propane tank filled. Propane…*what?* Even when I was drugged out or in drunken stupors and sleeping in strange men's homes, I never wound up in living conditions as rank as these! The amazing thing was that this excuse of a house was next door to Linda Goodman, the quite famous astrologer the boys followed.

We spent the first few nights in a motel until the utilities were turned on and while we painted and cleaned the inside of our new abode. We slept on futons on the floor of our bedrooms and Steve fabricated a couch frame with 2x4s. Every morning, I had to roll up my bed and drag it into the living room where it became an instant couch. I was so unreasonable about having to do this simple task. I worked hard at making every situation impossible. I just wanted to go back to my real home. I wanted to go back to Cincinnati. I stood fast against the flow of events and refused to be the adaptable Gemini I should have been. The boys did everything to make me comfortable, but I was miserable and made damn well certain that everyone around me was as well…even the cats. Plus, I couldn't take the nights—they were relentlessly quiet. I wasn't comfortable with no noise; it made me feel so alone with nothing to do. If all that weren't enough, I continued to be obsessed with the unfinished rocky romance with Sean back home. My thoughts bubbled like browning lasagna in my brain. I was getting downright nasty.

I decided to leave Cripple Creek, the cats, and the boys after three weeks. I bought a Greyhound bus ticket with the money I'd borrowed from Paula back in Cincinnati. Kitty had to stay with the boys because Greyhound does not haul animals. As the bus pulled out of the terminal from Colorado

Springs for the thirty-six-hour ride to Cincinnati, I had a terrible feeling of anguish grip my gut. It was a familiar sensation which I immediately related to other events in my past when I was doing something that was bad for me.

I knew I was totally going against my intuition by going back to Sean—but I refused to listen to it. I hated that I allowed myself to be pulled back into the arms of my crackpot boyfriend. I wasn't in love with him. I didn't trust him. Quite honestly, I don't even think I liked him. I blamed Rob and Steve for my misery, even though they had nothing to do with it. They were sick about my unhappiness and about my co-dependent relationship with Sean, but I was overpowered by the whole thing. There was no talking to me. In the end, it had ripped the three of us apart.

I stayed with Sean for the first few weeks of my return, but after a series of trashy-traileresque boyfriend drama scenes, I finished the dance with the alcoholic menace in my life...this time, for good. Paula flew over in her trusty Suzuki Samurai when I called her and screamed, "Enough is enough!" She helped me move the few belongings I had and me back into David Wilson's apartment. After going through a couple of job snippets, I wound up as a waitress in a cool place downtown called The Bistro. I eventually rented the apartment across the hall from David's (our apartments were the only two on the third and top floors and we called them The Penthouse Suites).

Nine months later, the boys and the cats returned from Cripple Creek, and between David's pad and mine, they had two places they could hang their babushkas and call home. Fortunately, the fabric of our friendship was restored to its full, durable strength. But even so, with all the commotion I caused in my life (and others) I still never gave a thought as to why I let myself settle for zero when men were involved. If my friends treated me like both boyfriends had, they would no longer have been my friends. I wouldn't stand for friends I couldn't trust or didn't respect me — so why a lover?

MY BAGS ARE PACKED AND I'M READY TO GO

Saturn Return. This astrological event happens in everyone's life. Saturn is called the "Father Planet" for many reasons. It denotes the energy of responsibility and karma. Saturn Return is a masculine voice pushing you and saying, "Look at your life, look at the responsibility, or lack thereof. What needs to change? What do you want to do?" These returns are on a seven-year cycle (that's where the term "seven-year itch" came from) but the strongest cycles happen every twenty-eight years.

Late 1989 — I was twenty-eight years old (hmmm!) and had been living in Cincinnati for five years (not counting those three lost weeks in Colorado). I loved it here, but felt there was more for me to do than what I was doing. I had a keen apartment, a fun job at The Bistro, and it was in this city where I was enveloped by the love of wondrous people that I learned I was absolutely worthwhile. But I was on edge, longing to make myself more than I was. For the first time, I started to look toward my future. I was reconciling myself to the fact that a man wasn't going to take care of me and I would have to do it myself. I felt I might never marry and I was certain I didn't want to have children. I was also positive that I didn't want to be a waitress for the rest of my life. Beyond that, however, I didn't know what I wanted to do. Maybe try school again? A trade school? A real stab at acting and singing? I decided to move back to Tucson to confront my past and to try and figure me out. I wasn't afraid of myself in Tucson anymore and I wasn't on the run from something. This time, I was running *towards* something.

It was settled. My parents were expecting me, and Paula was going to take a vacation to see the West and slow the car down long enough to drop me off in Tucson. It was less than a month before exodus when I ran into an old friend I hadn't seen since Rusconi days. We made plans for dinner before my return to the desert. The night we went out, he revealed that his godmother had passed away and willed him a small bar, a beer-'n-shot pub, she and her late husband had owned in downtown Cincinnati for some thirty-odd years. After we finished eating, he wanted me to see it.

Walking into *Lee Chesnuts' Hideaway* near the corner of 8th and Main Streets in downtown Cincinnati was traveling back in time. As soon as the door opened with a slap-in-the-face cloud of cigarette smoke, I saw a "Do Not Enter With Firearms" sign above the old, once-lustrous mahogany bar. The only window in the joint was a small rectangle close to the ceiling, but Pabst Blue Ribbon and Michelob neon signs obstructed the tiny bit of light that tried to sneak in. Stale beer, mildew, and a schnozzle-sting of body odors held the stagnant air hostage. The drop ceiling, suspended by coat hangers in some places, was corn-flaked and yellowed with nicotine and chili grease. The jukebox loudly twanged Hank Williams, Sr., mourning lost love of a pickup truck or perhaps a girlfriend.

The furnishings were a mix of the worst picks from a down-and-out thrift store—nothing matched and all had been torn and patched with anything from cellophane to packaging tape and, in some places, staples. (I found out about the staples when I sat on one.) The springs in the seats of the two round vinyl booths in the back of the pub were so "bounceless" that when I plopped down in one, I felt like I was sitting in a bagel hole.

The toilet in the men's room had been removed from the wall many moons ago and replaced with a five-gallon pickle bucket. No sink. The condom machine was still on the wall, but was broken. The women's room had a toilet underneath muck, with a patched wall and floor of Formica, particleboard, and linoleum; and there was a corroded sink that dribbled only cold water, but no soap, mirrors, or towel dispenser. And there was a dented metal trash can.

I sat at the bar and tried to imagine what this place must have looked like decades ago—alive with laughter, card games, and good ol' boys and saucy dames in hats. The atmosphere and clientele today, however, were as lifeless and broken down as the environment, except for the intruding thunderclap of the bowling machine and one loud customer who was being refused service until he settled his bar bill from the previous month. I could see his anger rising and the veins pounding in his temples. In half a second, an old metal barstool whizzed by my head and I hit the floor. After the barstool thrower was removed from the premises and the ruckus reduced to a steady beer-sipping murmur, I pried myself from the red, black, and cigarette-sizzled carpet. I was probably safer sitting upright with my cranium in harm's way of flying furniture than dealing with the variety of skin rashes I might have contracted from this contaminated polyester-blend floor covering.

My friend drove me home soon afterwards and I didn't know how to congratulate him on his new enterprise. He had won the prize. I mean, this was the armpit of all dives! I thought that if my godmother had left me that dumpster, she would have been repaying me for something I'd done to her when I was a child.

The next morning, I received a ring on the telephone bright and early. (In the world of restaurants, early means before noon.) It was my friend from the previous evening's rendezvous offering me a proposition I could barely imagine.

ACT I
The Show

ONE HUNDRED PENNIES

The conversation went something like this: "Carol, I don't want it. I want to move to Boston in a year or so. I want nothing to do with the bar business ever again."

Fred had recently owned a nightclub with some other partners, but that venture had failed. All of the once-trusted alliances and friendships had been dragged out and gutted. Everybody had sued everybody else, leaving all with a sour taste in their mouths.

"But I grew up in this bar. My sisters and brothers did, too," he continued. "It used to be a great place. I don't want to see it close. If anyone can make it work, it's you. You know so many people."

He was right. After all, hadn't I been the Mayor of Newkirk Avenue in Brooklyn?

But hold up here! He wanted me to buy this joint? How and with what? My voluptuously good looks? My superb manners? Knowing which fork out of an eight-piece table setting to use for salad? I couldn't even offer to sleep with him because he'd rather sleep with my brother…if I had one. And wait a minute — I'd been a waitress and a bartender all my life. I didn't know how to run a business or manage people! I didn't even have a checkbook, a savings account, or a credit card. Hell, I didn't even have a Blockbuster card!

"As you can see, it needs a lot of work. I'll sell it to you for a dollar. And I'll help you remodel it."

What? A dollar?? One buck…one hundred pennies? That's all? I knew Fred was familiar with construction. Prior to the nightclub fiasco, he was involved with his family's drywall business — at least before that, too, went sour. He was a nice guy with bad business karma, but a nice guy.

How could this be happening to me? I was supposed to move to Arizona in a few weeks. I intended to stay there for a while and then move back to Cincy when the time was right. All my particleboard shelving and my Queen Anne cocktail table were in storage or at friends' homes to use while I was away. Even Kitty had packed her small Kitty-Carry-All, and the Paula Pony Express was ready to trot me out West. Mom was waiting for me, too, and Dad? Well, he was almost looking forward to seeing me.

After considerable thought and after weighing everything at least a hundred ways that I could possibly think of and without a single, solitary bit of know-how regarding business, I called Fred two days later and told him I wanted to be a bar owner. Sometimes offerings are just thrown in your lap, without knowing the reason why. The decision of what to do with them then is yours. I concluded this offering was meant to be. I thought this was the reason I had come back from Colorado.

Fred told me he'd sell me the joint for the sum of one dollar and stay around for a year or so until I got on my feet. He also said he had lots of people who could help (I stupidly assumed that help meant free) with the major electrical and plumbing work. My family of friends were right behind me — Rob, Steve, and close pal Greg were in my arena, and Paula kept chanting, "Don't let what you don't know now stop you!" All of that just fired me up more. Cautious David Wilson was also jubilant, but advised me to get a lawyer involved for my protection. Every time David mentioned that part, I'd shrug it off. Although I was convinced that this was my fate, I also felt it might easily be too good to be true, but I shrugged that off, too. The longing and edginess from wanting more for me were being quenched. This was my chance to be something *special* as Mom always said I'd be.

What an incredible opportunity — a chance of a lifetime. After all, how many people get to buy a bar for a buck? This is the stuff about which screenplays are written! Since I was a kid, I'd always known I was going to be famous. I just knew that this was my first stepping stone to get there. Even if I was just famous in Cincinnati, that would be fine with me! A golden door had just swung wide open and an ocean of light spilled through. I was twenty-eight years old already and if I didn't try, I'd never know. Besides, Fred wouldn't swindle me. He was a good-hearted, generous person and a fabulous tipper and drove an expensive sports car. Over the years, he'd taken groups of friends (myself included) out in chauffeured limousines to dine in gourmet restaurants and then signed the dinner checks to his account. The man bought his close gal-pals mink coats and diamond earrings. He wore tailor-made suits, fur coats, was always traveling, and carried a thick wad of cash. I figured he must have a bundle, right?

But why would somebody sell a bar and all the furnishings and the liquor license for a dollar? Maybe he wanted to give me this opportunity like—you know—a mentor would do. Maybe he just wanted to be the big man who could say, "I helped her get started." True, he may have been a bit of a talker, dropping names and boasting about splurging fifteen grand at posh restaurants for his company's Christmas parties; but it never occurred to me that such extravagance just might be one of the reasons he'd had two businesses and that both had failed.

But I was going to do it. I hadn't a clue how, but I was going to do it!

Fred's godmother had an apartment directly across the street from the place and he had been staying there off and on since her death. We figured it would be a good thing for me to live a scoodle away from my new bar so I could always keep an eye on it. Kitty and I moved out of the Penthouse and situated ourselves in the orange shag carpeted, light brown paneled apartment above an attorney's office.

Fred closed *Lee Chesnuts' Hideaway* in February 1990 and put a sign in the window that read "Closed for Remodeling." I had no idea who was going to do the remodeling or when it would begin. And though all of that was a little unnerving, it didn't matter. My anticipation of what would be was on fast-forward. I told The Bistro of my new plans, saying that I would be leaving in the near future to tend to my own business.

While I waitressed, I told all my customers about my new enterprise and gathered addresses for grand opening announcements. But I didn't stop there. I gathered them everywhere I went. Nothing like a little shameless self-promotion! I received mostly applause about my endeavor, but I did run into a few bulldog skeptics. I couldn't wait until the day came when they would step into my place and I could be smug and proud. I knew what I was capable of. I actually visualized it, seeing hordes of humans cramming to get in. I heard the music, I saw the people. I knew it was going to be a success.

Using numerology, Paula, Rob, Steve, and I thought of a name for this baby, and Rob and Steve formulated an astrological chart for her birth. Before they began researching a date, they asked me what I wanted the place to be—what I wanted it to represent. I knew.

Fun. Acceptance. Change. Love. Harmony. Family.

With my goals in mind, in the Gemini sun on Summer Solstice June 21st 1990 at 11:08 A.M., *Carol's Corner Café* would open its doors to the public.

OUT OF THE WOODWORK

This story is dedicated to Michael Lloyd Mueller—the ultimate Bette Davis fan who died in 1996 at the too young age of thirty-one from AIDS-related complications.

Fred said construction would begin at *Carol's* around the first of March, but it didn't. I had planned to work at The Bistro until the end of March and then visit my family for a few weeks in April before things got really nutty. Besides, Nancy had popped out another baby for this Earth—Ellissa, my only niece—and I hadn't met her yet. When I left for the Grand Canyon State, the bar remained untouched.

Fred told me that when I returned around the first of May, I would find my bar in the beginning phases of construction. I returned. It wasn't, and I quickly found myself getting more nervous. Although I knew nothing about this type of work, it was obvious that I was already behind schedule. I called Fred and learned that I was the demolition and construction crew…along with him. I guess he forgot to tell me. All he had said was that it would start soon. He neglected to inform me that it was up to me when it would start. We started the next day.

Rob Frommer (a fellow employee from The Bistro and a good friend) wanted to help. We hauled out the broken booths, chairs, and tables. We tore down the drop ceiling, ripped out the old plumbing, and threw that damned pickle bucket away. We lifted up three layers of carpeting and two layers of linoleum before we hit the original wood floor that looked like Saddam Hussein had thrown a party for a band of terrorists on it. I learned how to tile and grout the floor (all twelve hundred square feet of it). I also learned how to install and patch drywall. Damnation should come to the person who etched his name on one of my walls!

Rob, Steve, and Greg spent hours painting, cleaning, and drywalling, and when they weren't able to spend time in the place, they would at least drop by for a moment to lend emotional support. Michael Mueller was another angel who was sent to me. He was out of a job and wanted to be a waiter at *Carol's*. But before he made a dime serving, he worked his tuchis off for bologna sandwiches and beer doing everything and anything to get *Carol's* open.

On the outside, we pulled off the fake brick front that was popular in the 1960s and discovered the gingerbread wood-work of the late 1800s. The wood had been painted ten times over and it was finger-crippling work getting it down to the natural wood. Then we found a spot between the columns where a six-foot square window used to be. Perfect! That meant lots of light and openness.

One day, I was outside performing a balancing act on an unstable ladder, with a heat gun in my left hand and putty knife in my right. I was stripping off layer after layer of lead-based paint when I heard the screech of car brakes.

"Carol Sherman! What the hell are *you* doing up there?"

I recognized the voice immediately. It belonged to Bill Lindenschmidt, my good friend and customer from Rusconi's who'd driven the truck the day I moved out of Tim's house.

Bill reported my plans to his business partner Sue Noble, also a former Rusconi-ite. They owned a wood refinishing company and twenty-four hours later, Bill, Sue, and Sue's girl-friend Sandy Warner came by with a troop of more friends and offered their assistance…their *free* assistance. They wanted to do whatever it took to get my place in beautiful condition. Working into the wee hours of the morning when nobody else was around, they sanded, stained, and varnished the beaten, mahogany bar and restored its dignity. When their work was completed, this once-abused furnishing looked like it belonged in a swank, big city club of the 1940s!

Paula performed countless errands and tasks—she painted walls, ran to the hardware store a thousand times, and helped me address, lick, and stamp over three hundred invitations for the pre-opening parties. But the most intense job she did was using ammonia to clean the smelly, fungus-covered, walk-in refrigerator. Several thousand brain cells evaporated out of her head and she was high for days. While she's no longer high, we're all convinced that the brain cells never returned.

The most amazing thing about this whole endeavor was the friendship. People I had worked with at other restaurants came by to help and they brought their friends. Everyone was genuinely happy for me. Folks I hadn't seen in years came out of the woodwork to give their time. They'd seen me work from bar to bar and restaurant to restaurant and they wanted something good to happen for me. I felt as though they were celebrating me as if I were the poster girl for the American dream: LOCAL WAITRESS MAKES GOOD! I had no idea that I was loved so much. *Just what do people see in me that I don't see in myself? Why do they like me so much? What have I given them that makes them want to give in return?*

With the exception of the plumbing, electrical, and heating/air conditioning, all the work that went into building my new establishment was love-labor. Everyone wanted to be a part of the process. In a way, it was like an Amish barn raising. Every day, friends and acquaintances, customers, and fellow employees put in an hour or two or three or sometimes a lot more of manual labor before and/or after work. People brought food and drink. The warmth I felt was beyond words. This place wouldn't have been built without them.

To purchase the materials and supplies needed, to buy permits and rent dumpsters, to have plumbing and electrical work completed required capital, of which I had none. In fact, I didn't have a dime. Because it was never discussed and I was too ignorant to know any better, I had assumed my wealthy friend Fred would take care of it. At least, that's the impression I got. I mean, he knew I didn't have money. I hadn't a clue how much money was needed for this kind of stuff. Then came his tales of business woes.

It seems he didn't have any money, either. In fact, after his drywall company went belly-up, the family had started a new business and now that company was also in the process of going down the tubes. As he told me this, his car phone was being repossessed because the company hadn't paid the bill. I ended up having to beg and borrow (but not steal) to continue construction. I borrowed $2,500 from Uncle Robert and some funds from my parents. I had no idea that my poverty-stricken friend Fred had borrowed money from his family and friends to assist with *my* entrepreneurial endeavor until he handed me the cash and told me how much I owed whom. That's where the "dream" started to get weird.

Using as excuses my own lack of business sense and the deficit of communication between Fred and me, I could have walked away a month into construction. We were only three weeks from opening. I was in over my head. But with that much hard labor and planning behind me and my visualization of my own place, I *knew* I had to do this. I had to make it happen. I was convinced that all my friends had been sent by the Universe to help me, and I couldn't let them—or me—down. I was doing something for me and for the first time my life, I was doing something significant.

HOW HIGH THE URINAL?

Even having never been involved in construction before, I sensed that the manner in which the troops of volunteers were being led by Fred (who had simply assumed the position of job foreman) wasn't the way it should have been. Things weren't completed in order, and often work was ripped out because something else needed to have been completed first. We had no lists or schedules to work from, so we were forever running for materials. He was full of good ideas and inexpensive ways of constructing things, but all were worthless when not thought through (or found illegal because of building codes). Insufficient planning wasted a lot of time and too often, we needlessly spent money twice.

When the plumbers came to install the bathroom fixtures, one of the exposed-butt-crack dudes walked up to me and asked me how high I wanted the urinal to be mounted on the wall. Now how the hell was I supposed to know that? Couldn't he test it himself? He had better knowledge about urinal height than I did. I dropped to my knees directly in front of him, raised my right hand to my mouth. "Mount it that high," I said and walked away.

These small missiles that exploded were merely "poofs" compared to the bomb Fred dropped next. He told me he was leaving for a couple of weeks to go to Philadelphia for a deposition regarding a lawsuit with one of the defunct businesses. Since he needed to prepare for his trip, he wouldn't be around for the last part of the pre-opening parties or the grand opening on June 21st. I was on my own. Just my friends and I would open this business. I was relieved that I had them, and also that my mother was coming to town. But I was still terrified.

I planned twelve pre-opening parties. An hour before the first party, Rob and Steve demanded that I put down the paintbrush and go home to shower. The truck that held my twenty very late barstools had just parked in front and they helped unload and uncrate them. They were opening the last box when I arrived back on the scene, just as the invited guests walked across the wet-paint threshold of *Carol's*. Some guests helped crush the boxes and carry them outside to a dumpster. *Family is already happening*, I thought to myself.

I had several noon parties to let the downtown business people know that *Carol's* served lunch, and I held happy hour parties for other crowds. The most fun and demanding parties were the late-nighters that didn't begin until 11:00 p.m. These were the ones for our fellow restaurant workers. I wanted them to know they had a great place to relax and party after work. All the socials went fairly smoothly and were well attended. Paula was there for most of the parties, exchanging her bartending expertise for champagne. David Wilson left a restaurant where he had worked for several years and came to tend bar at *Carol's*. I hired Rob and Steve as bartenders as well. Complimentary hot appetizers that were on the new menu were served in chafing pans borrowed from The Bistro. New customers bought cocktails which helped to aid the negative cash flow; but these dollars were still like using a slotted spoon to dredge water from a half-submerged Titanic.

Before Fred left for Philadelphia, he showed me how to write checks and left a list of food and beverage purveyors to call to get deliveries. Because Rob Frommer was familiar with ordering food, he made a chart and an inventory list that contained all the spices, meats, canned goods, and other items that comprised *Carol's* menu. Rob held my hand while he taught me how to order. He also helped me interview prospective cooks, and how he laughed during the first interview when my opening question was, "What's your astrological sign?" I hadn't even given training a thought until a few days before when

Rob asked me *when* and *how* these people were going to be trained. I wouldn't have known what to do without Rob. I had only recently learned how to make brewed coffee, so training people to cook was way beyond my skill level.

After all the pre-opening parties and on the evening before the grand opening, I was a physical and mental mess. I was stressed to the max, hadn't slept in days, and my ears were infected from the drywall dust. Rob told Mom I was useless and to put me to bed while he trained the two cooks we'd hired. So on his orders, I went home where I took a long, hot shower and put on my comfy Betty Boop sleep shirt. My mother came over and tucked me in, pulled the covers under my chin, stroked my face, and kissed me on the forehead. "Goodnight darling," she said. "I'm *so* proud of you. Now get some sleep because you have a *big* day tomorrow," as if I were a girl starting the first day of kindergarten. Then she went back across the street to wash dishes. I tried to sleep, but I couldn't keep my eyes closed. I got out of bed, sat on the window ledge in my new apartment that looked directly at my new restaurant, pulled my old Kitty close to my chest, lit a cigarette and thought, *What the hell did I get myself into?*

COME OVER TO MY HOUSE!

Since the purple neon sign that should have been proudly announcing *Carol's Corner Café* wasn't ready for the grand opening, the thirteen lunch customers had no clue about where they were dining. They had just seen the work that was being done over the past seven weeks and were curious about this new place. In order to dispel any confusion, Mom filled them in. As she glided from table to table shaking hands and giving out handwritten menus on legal pad paper (because the printer didn't have the laminated menus on time), Mom enlightened everyone: "Hello! Welcome to *Carol's Corner Café*! *I'm* Carol's mother!" Though the thirteen guests didn't know who Carol was, they were still charmed!

We did it. The first lunch was under our belt...and I was still alive.

It was a rough morning. The sunken-faced, little Italian man with a gray handlebar mustache who wished to be called Chef Roberto decided not to come into work on opening day. Chef Roberto was a decent short-order cook, but he was a far stretch from being considered a chef. I'd hired him to crank out the complementary eats for the preview parties and to work days thereafter. Someone came over and told me that he was just a "stoned-throw" away. We went out the front door, made a left to the back of the building, and found him lying in the alley amongst the pigeon poop and grease, dead drunk and hugging a bottle of Mad Dog 20/20 wrapped in a crumpled paper bag. This is when I *should have* learned not to give pay advances. Thank God for Rob Frommer who once again came to my rescue and worked lunch that day...and the day after that...and the day after that.

With or without the designated cook for the day, *Carol's* was a success from the minute she opened her doors. I say "she" because there was no separation between the restaurant and me. I soon became one of her biggest draws...and largest of detriments. I'd been absent from Rusconi's for about three years and all my clientele had waited for another incarnation. They all came and brought more friends.

It was perfect timing. *Hmmm*...imagine that.

Owning my own business forced me to learn some management and people skills, plus I got crash courses on reality as a bonus. I consider myself street smart and a good reader of people, but I was awed at the times I trusted and shouldn't have (or didn't trust and should have).

For instance, during the fourth month I was open, an infrequent customer came in on a Saturday afternoon and bought a burger, fries, and a beer and paid for it with a $100 dollar traveler's check. He received ninety-two bucks and some change back in cash. Then I looked at the check and noticed it was countersigned in a woman's name. When I asked him about it, he quickly responded that when he had purchased the money, he was in drag. I went into my office (which used to be a coat closet), sat down at my desk (which Rob Frommer had made by sawing a sewing machine table in half), and called American Express and learned that the checks had been stolen. When I went back out to confront him, the double-dealer had departed. I prowled the streets, but he was nowhere.

I didn't get to feeling *too* moronic until I laid the story out to the police fraud squad, gave them a description of the schlemiel, and said I wanted to press charges. They cackled like old hens. "He said *what* to you? And you believed *that*? Come over here, Carol, and tell him the story! He won't believe this! Joe, you gotta listen to this one!" I'm glad they were amused. When the trial came about a few weeks later, the thief was a no-show because he was locked up in a mental hospital. This is how I learned most of my lessons.

I ran *Carol's Corner Café* by trial and error—sometimes trial before a lynch mob. I had no knowledge of accounting, business, taxes, comparative shopping, managing, firing, hiring, or advertising. I stumbled more often than not, but owning a business started to give me some backbone. Having never known my niche in life, I was as revved up as a hot rod. I finally knew that I was good at *something* — I was a great front person. I loved making everyone feel comfortable and welcome, shooting out jokes and funnies, making them laugh. I talked to everyone — even the people I didn't like — and made sure they left happy. With the instant customer success, I knew I was doing *something* right. I, Carol Sherman, was making a difference. I had created something that Cincinnati had been yearning for. *Carol's* wasn't just a bar or restaurant — it was like a social gathering in my living room, except that my friends paid for their drinks.

Cincinnati has a lot of money, a lot of old money, and it is known as a conservative town. I was fed up to the tip of my head chakra knowing that gays and lesbians had only dingy places to party, eat, and drink. Why were the city's gay bars smoke-filled basements with dirty bathrooms and no windows (and if these bars do have windows, why are they tinted?) Why aren't there more places like Rusconi's?

This is how I made my mark in Cincinnati with *Carol's Corner Café*. A screaming huge window in the front of the place, clean bathrooms, a variety of music on a state-of-the-art jukebox, good food at decent prices, cocktails with a kick, and a fantastic array of human beings together under one roof. Everyone was welcome at *Carol's*. It was home.

Within months, I paid Uncle Robert and my parents back, and also the people I didn't know from whom Fred had borrowed money. David Wilson was promoted to bar manager and Greg (whom I'd gotten close to and had been best friends with Rob Dorgan since the first grade) joined our ranks as a waiter and bartender. Fred did help me in many ways. He escorted me to an attorney to become incorporated about five weeks after opening. I hadn't a clue that this needed to be done. We established a corporate minute book showing me as the sole owner of one hundred shares of stock that was transferred from *Lee Chesnuts' Hideaway* to the incorporated name of *Carol's Corner Café, Inc.* I signed legal documents naming me president, vice president, secretary, and treasurer of my corporation (Fred's name wasn't on any of these documents), and then we exchanged one dollar in front of the attorney for the sale of the business. Before Fred took the money, the attorney asked him if he was absolutely certain that he didn't want anything out of my business, and he said that he didn't.

Fred taught me how to do payroll, sales tax, and some other fundamentals of Business 101. Unfortunately, he didn't always teach me the correct methods. He bartended with me on weekend nights when he was in town and ran errands for the place. If something broke (the unwritten law of restaurants states that at least one thing will break every twenty-four hours), he would "spit and glue" it or find someone who could. As the months went on, however, I realized that he wanted to control me, from the way I dressed, down to my hair color. It wasn't any of his business, although my loyalty to him for giving me this opportunity kept my mouth shut.

Okay, it wasn't just some misguided loyalty that harnessed my tongue. He was stronger and much more powerful than I was. As I got to know more about his former and present interactions with business associates, ex-friends, and family, I learned that he routinely threatened and pursued lawsuits, used intimidation tactics, and was downright vindictive. Fred told me how he absolutely loved dragging people into court, even when he knew his chances of winning were small. He admitted that even if he ended up losing a lawsuit, he took pleasure in knowing that at least the defending side would learn a lesson by having to shell out money for attorneys and wasting precious time. The more I learned about him, the more frightened I became. I didn't want to rock the boat.

He drank a lot and, in my opinion, took too much prescription medicine that always seemed to be readily available in a small "drugstore" in the back of his car. I'd catch him in lies that he'd make up about things that meant absolutely nothing. Every so often, he'd go off on crying jags and tantrums, claiming that soon I wouldn't need him around anymore because I was learning how to take care of business by myself. He became more and more possessive of me and said that I should never marry because whatever slouch I wound up with would take advantage of me and hurt my business. Fred still had his charming and loving ways; but the more I did things on my own and the more I didn't follow his advice, the more peculiar he acted. I had the same sense of impending doom as I had when I allowed Deidra to run my life.

THAR'S GOLD IN THEM THAR MOUNTAINS!

I believe in astrology. I don't sign any important document until I have an astrological chart made. I believe death is a crossover to a different form of life, that the Earth is not the only planet in our galaxy inhabited by intelligent beings, and I'm a stout believer in karma. I listen to my dreams, try to interpret them, and believe in the healing power of mind and minerals. Whether it be good or bad, I believe everything happens for a reason and that there are no coincidences. Some people find my beliefs a bunch of hocus-pocus bullshit, but they work for me. I'm very liberal (my father said I take after

my mom, the bleeding heart of America) and feel that people
have the right to believe or do anything they wish, as long as
it's not harmful to others. But Fred really threw me when he
told me the old story that entwines truth with myth about millions of dollars in lost gold in the Superstition Mountains outside Phoenix, Arizona. According to the legend, the gold from
the Lost Dutchman's Mine was supposedly stolen from a pack
train by Apaches and hidden in the mountains over a hundred
years ago.

Fred claimed that in a past life, he was one of the robbers
and that he knew where the treasure was hidden and he was
going west to get it. He told me before he left for Arizona that
if he found the gold, he would call me with some sort of code
and fill me in. My job was to hire a private helicopter that
would meet him on the mountain to pick up the shiny millions.
He gave me explicit instructions not to tell anyone and to
swear the pilot to secrecy about the wealth that his aircraft was
to transport. Fred would give the flyer a good sum of cash for
his services and this would buy his silence. His reason for total
privacy was that he didn't want the IRS or the government to
know he'd found the fortune because, since it didn't belong to
him in the first place, he might have to return it. Even if he
were allowed to keep it, he said, it would be taxed out the
wazoo. How could I possibly argue with that?

He took his trip to Arizona (which I paid for), but he was-
n't able to put his greedy fingers on the gold. A lot of rain put
a damper on his mountain excursions. I was just happy to get
him out of my hair for a few weeks, even though it was becoming clear to me that he wasn't acting rationally. Unfortunately,
he held something very important over my head that I knew he
would use to his full advantage. The liquor license for *Carol's*

was still in his dead godmother's name and under the title of *Lee Chesnuts' Hideaway*.

I was afraid if I told him I could run my own business and for him to get his own life, he wouldn't pursue the transfer of the license. Because *Lee Chesnuts* was willed to Fred in a power of attorney, the license had to be transferred into his name before it could be transferred into mine. If he felt threatened in any way, he would probably take off with his permit, and I had worked too hard for that to happen. A liquor license is not just something one can go shopping for to replace, especially where *Carol's* was located. In that zone, the Department of Liquor Control was restricting newer permits because they felt the downtown area was becoming saturated with liquor licenses. Besides, where would I get the kind of money needed to buy one?

Why didn't I seek a lawyer's advice? All the business people associated with *Carol's*, such as the accountant, the liquor license attorney, and the corporate lawyer were long-time buddies and business associates of Fred. He always spoke of the special friendship they shared and how they would do anything for him. I felt trapped. So in October 1990 when he asked me to pay him $500 a week with no time restrictions, I put my tail between my legs and did so. Fred suggested I write "loan payment" on the memo line of the check. Although I hadn't borrowed money from him, he said that way he wouldn't be taxed. I wasn't savvy or shrewd enough to find other alternatives to this predicament except to play it cool and pray he would disappear from my life forever when he moved to Boston.

COME DOWNTOWN: THE PARKING'S A BUCK, BUT THE ENTERTAINMENT'S FREE!

I have definitely met more than my share of left-of-center humans. Don't get me wrong, I'm not complaining. Without them, I would just be a lonely little Jewish girl wandering aimlessly through life searching for the ultimate bargain. The lefties are Cincinnati's finest, not the "boys in blue." These are the locals who add spurts of color to the downtown ambiance.

In my years of working downtown, I had the pleasure of encountering people like:

The man who walked backwards. For no apparent reason (at least to us), this man walked backwards wherever he went. He'd walk forward a few steps then half-spin in mid-stride and continue backwards, glide a few yards, half-spin, then forward face again. He was painfully thin, about mid-thirties, pale gray in color, bent over from the waist, with his fingers tucked into the front pockets of his pants showing only his bony knuckles. His back was so bowed it looked like a sideways U, but when he made his half rotation to assume retrograde, he was like a ballerina in a pirouette, very graceful, up on his toes, and twirling with ease.

The lady who talked to her cigarettes. Sometimes she screamed at them, sometimes she tried to feed them. She would bite their filters off and spit them to the ground as if she were sucking poison out of a viper-stricken body part. Why she didn't buy non-filtered cigs to begin with baffled me; but who knows, she may have had a motive for this ritual. Caucasian, short, and petite in frame, she walked with her elbows tight into her sides like they were screwed, holding her cigarette pack underneath her breasts as if she were cupping water. Miniskirts were her year-round attire and although she didn't have Betty Grable legs, hers weren't too bad. She could have been thirty-five, maybe forty-five. I couldn't tell. Her long, matted, brown hair was always draped over her face. She looked like Cousin It without sunglasses.

The tall skinny Black man who wore metallic-fabric "Sheik of Araby" get-ups. He wore a halo under which was tucked a pillowcase that fluttered behind him in the wind. Around his waist, he tied a rope belt, and his legs were so long that his gait must have been a good five-foot step. He carried a shepherd's staff and roamed the streets and alleys, calling out the time every hour on the dot like it was his consecrated task in life. But before he simulated Big Ben, he'd stand strong to the sidewalk and bang his staff on the concrete as if to capture the attention of passersby. He was pleasant and always acknowledged a greeting with a quick nod.

The thin Asian woman. She wore an ID badge on a length of colored yarn around her neck and carried a raggedy briefcase. Her black, greasy hair was parted in the middle but still hung in her face. Her knee socks always matched her ensemble. She looked worried and sad as she constantly jotted down scribbles on a small pad of paper. This woman rode buses all day, having nowhere to go but always in a rush nonetheless.

The construction clown. He was about fifty. A fairly plump man who wore clown suits with ruffled necks and big shoes (but no red nose). He toted a metal lunch box and wore a hard hat. Quite the happy guy, he stood by any construction site downtown and observed intently, smiling for hours upon hours. Just like the letter carrier, neither rain nor sleet nor snow would keep this clown from his self-appointed station. Greg's life ambition was to find out what was in that damn lunch box. He once caught the clown walking into an apartment building and waited almost an hour in his car, spying on which apartment lights went on. But alas, the clown must have lived in perpetual darkness.

THE MIDGETS IN MY LIFE – #2

I'd seen him roaming the streets, panhandling and yelling at cars. One day, Red decided to pay *Carol's* homage and hopped up on a barstool. This snippet was mangy looking, with beastly red, stringy hair, and a Rip Van Winkle beard. His clothes were ratty and his hands were filthy. There was more dirt under his fingernails than his entire cubic body weight and he smelled like a wet-dog that had just rolled in a sewer. Red looked mean. I wasn't sure if he really was or that's just the way he looked because his face was scrunched like a decaying jack-o'-lantern. Along with his body odor, I also smelled trouble and I sensed that his dismissal from my bar was inevitable. He asked for a Miller Lite. I gave him his beer, he gave me the money, and I resumed my conversation with my friends Rob and Steve and continued to tend my bar.

A few minutes later, a guest who was dining with his wife came to me and asked if I would please remove the "little man" who had made himself at home at their table and was being annoying. I politely asked Red to return to his barstool to finish his beer and not to talk to this couple. He looked mad and hurt, as though he'd been jilted (I guess in a way he was). He claimed that he was only making conversation, but he reluctantly obliged my request. I barely had time to return to my friends when the same irritated guest told me the midget had returned and was now saying rude things to his wife. This fulfilled my premonition of his removal from my estab-lishment and I sternly asked him to leave. He mumbled something under his breath, and barged outside in an angry munchkin march.

But before I knew it, the wee one returned. I didn't see him at first because the bar was taller than he was. In fact, the only way I knew he was there was that I heard him screaming at the top of his lungs in the middle of my dining room that *Carol's Corner* was prejudiced against midgets. I was really mad now. When he wouldn't leave on his own, I picked him up by the back of his collar and shoved him out onto the sidewalk just like in the cartoons. His miniature arms and legs thrashed through the air as if he were battery operated and short-cir-cuiting. What a stunt! I should have charged a cover.

Just when we thought all we had of Red were memories, we heard him returning. My bar was getting busier and I was frustrated about having to deal with him for another round. Rob, bless his heart, got up from the bar and told me he would take care of him once and for all. Rob restrained him from entering by blocking the doorway with his body and, in a peaceful and teacher-like way, told the bellicose bad boy, "Carol has asked you to leave several times. Now if you insist on coming in, we will be forced to call the cops and have you removed." Squinting his beady eyes that were lined with crust-ed sleep, Red yelled back at Rob, "I ain't afraid of no cops!" and tried to squirm his way into the restaurant. In order for Rob to be at eye-level with this stick of dynamite, he got down on his knees and screamed, "What about the wicked witch!"

Red's eyes bugged out and he ran into the street as fast as his little legs could hustle. He probably thought Rob was crazier than he was. Red, however, still wasn't done. He started gathering orange construction barrels and barricades from the street and used them to block the entrance to my place. He was such a determined and busy little bee, that I let him have his fun. Soon exhausted from all his labors, he disappeared into the dimly lit street and returning, I presume, to Oz.

MOM WAS RIGHT

I was too much for guys. Too loud, too opinionated, too liberal, too childish, too headstrong, too whatever. Many men were intimidated that I had my own business but even more of them couldn't deal with my lifestyle, my beliefs, or my gay friends. As two significant and several unimportant shammed relationships had failed, I couldn't see modifying myself to fit neat and tidy in some guy's realm. I hadn't always felt that way, however.

I used to starve myself, believing my weight was the problem. I used to tone myself down a notch or two, thinking my fireworks personality was the problem. I even used to try to camouflage my closeness with the gay community, in case that that was the problem. But these *weren't* problems. I couldn't change myself any more than RuPaul could change into a lesbian. I just simply hadn't met the right man.

I continued with the one-nighters but no longer held onto the illusion that I was going to find him that way. In fact, I had grown callous towards men and was simply jumping into the sack out of habit. It's what I expected of myself. It's all I knew. It wasn't until I had a particularly disgusting encounter with a partial human that my gears were jump-kicked to move forward and work on *myself*. I finally understood that I was selling myself short and to the lowest bidder. I suddenly realized that I deserved much, much more. Before this, I'd never thought of what I wanted in a man, I'd just grabbed and tried to keep most of the men who came anywhere near me. *Why is it such a struggle to like yourself and believe you're entitled to the best?* Anyway, that's when the healing and analyzing inner-self work commenced. I figured after I was right with myself that if love was meant for me, it would come to be.

During the renovation of my personal interior, I put the quest to discover Prince Charming behind me. I needed to focus on me. At thirty-one years of age, I was very comfortable with myself, understanding I might never marry and that I'd still have my business, my friends, my life work. I felt I could be quite conten.. with that. I decided to stop giving myself to every male who breathed and to wait for someone I really liked and to wait until I knew the feelings were reciprocated. Someone was going to have to respect me and love me—every aspect of me. That's what it's supposed to be about, right? To know the best and the worst things about someone and to love them for it anyway? Isn't that what people say true love is all about? How was anyone going to love me if I wore someone else's costume? It was a simple yet brilliant realization, although it hardly came to me overnight. It took a long time and it took lots of talks with close friends and family and most of all, lots of talks with me. I had to learn to love me. I know that's what everybody says you're supposed to do. But have you tried it? It's not as easy as it sounds! Anyway, until I was able to love myself, until I cleared my clouded vision, until I gave myself top billing…love wasn't going to happen.

When I *was* right with myself, I met a thirty-seven-year-old man who liked himself plenty and knew exactly what he wanted and with whom he wished to share his life.

MY DON

I knew something was up the second I met him. In late September 1992, I went with Sue and Sandy to see k.d. lang in concert. Afterwards, they dropped me off at a watering hole called Local 1207, a place up on Main Street that used to be a premier blues club. This was during the Clinton-Bush election campaign and on the lapel of my jacket, I wore a button with the name BUSH with a big red slash through it. This guy asked me if I was making a political statement or a personal one. I said both. We laughed and it was kismet.

In October, we went on our first date. We went out to dinner and then to his house to carve pumpkins. I knew this was a man who was always prepared, and not just because I eyed the Baggie of moistened towelettes in his car but also because as I walked into his home, I saw that he had everything laid out on the cocktail table in the living room:

1. a choice round pumpkin resting on top of a drop cloth

2. a brand new pumpkin carving kit with several spooky patterns to choose from

3. several pens to draw the pattern on the pumpkin

4. another drop cloth under the table

5. large spoons to scoop out the pumpkin guts

6. a medium-sized garbage can lined with a plastic bag

7. a bottle of delicious red wine, candles, and romantic music

I could tell my date was uneasy watching me draw the outline of a scary cat on the pumpkin. He didn't allow my hard work to go without his offering a few tips along the way. *This man takes his squash quite seriously*, I thought to myself. When it came time for the incisions, I knew to steer clear. I just sat back and watched. His carving was so precise that it literally took hours…three, to be exact. Neurosurgeons take less time rewiring brains! I fell asleep on the couch but was abruptly awakened by the roar of a motor. He was vacuuming the pumpkin droppings I'm sure I was responsible for.

I thought he was on drugs. Only people doing large amounts of cocaine act like this. It was four o'clock in the friggin' morning and he was vacuuming pumpkin poop off the carpet. How was I going to explain my new boyfriend to my mother? Look, Ma, I want you to meet my new man…he's a regular June Cleaver with testicles. I truly wondered if he was straight. Such thoughts, however, were fleeting. After the carpet was clean, we lit the candle in the pumpkin and engaged in our first kiss. I didn't ever want our lips to part. When he drove me home, we had to wait for a train to pass on the tracks, which gave us more time to kiss. After eight years of wedlock, I still hope for a train to cross when we're in the car together!

The kisser's name is Donald P. Jones. He normally goes by Don, but his long-time buddies call him Donnie. The length of our marriage has already surpassed his two previous marriages combined. I wonder what the two ex-Mrs. Jones didn't see that I see. Why the heck would anyone *not* want to stay married to this man? Perhaps Don had some coming-of-age to do, growing, discovering himself, coming into his own—similar to what I had to go through. If we'd met earlier in our lives, I know I wouldn't have had the wisdom, knowledge, or love for myself that I did when the Universe finally brought us together. I was still baking, still searching for me, and we might not have been ready for each other.

Before getting hitched, I told Don that I was going to confer with Rob and Steve for the astrological birthday for our marriage. He and I discussed what we wanted our marriage to be and I took this information to the boys. They helped us decide the date and time of our wedding. When making the arrangements for our ceremony at the temple, the rabbi asked us what time we should begin. I told him the ceremony should start at 10:16 a.m. The rabbi asked why such a precise time, and Don chimed, "Carol has astrological beliefs we must follow." No doubt about it, I'd met the right one.

Don is comfortable and secure with himself and hasn't any negative issues with my gay friends or my commitment and attachment with the gay community. He unblinkingly invites my HIV positive friends into our home (all my friends and family are welcomed by my man). He's proud of the benefits I do for AIDS charities and my picketing for justice and equality with civil rights organizations. He'd paint my picket signs, if I needed him to. In the early phases of our relationship, Don was cornered by a business associate who told him that his company might lose some cash flow because I owned a gay bar. Don told him that if that happened, he didn't need that type of client. He is not intimidated and doesn't play those games. Never has been. As Don showed Rob and Steve around our digs before they house-sat for us while we vacationed, he walked the boys into our bedroom. "This is where you guys will sleep." Plain, matter-of-fact, validating the boys are as much a couple as we are.

I know the Universe planned our union. Don needs to nurture, coddle, and take care of someone, while at the same time retaining *his* independence. He also needs to know that he is the zenith in my life. That's easy. He is. Don knows that I must go my own way and do my own thing for me to be whole. Don doesn't want me to breathe solely for him. He doesn't want that burden. Besides, he knows I have other desires and demands for myself just as he has for himself. My Don plays with the child inside of me with attention and warmth, and he also gratifies the woman in me. He feeds my creativity and helps to spark my ideas into reality. And if they flop, he helps me figure out why, kicks me in the butt, and then urges me to try again.

When I told him I was going to write a book, he bought a program for our computer that would help me with my endeavor and taught me how to use it. When I wanted to take a writing class, he sent me to school. When I wanted to audition for "Fiddler on the Roof," he said, "Do it, baby!" And when I landed the part of Yente, he helped me with my lines and invited the world to see the play. He likes building me. He wants me to be all I'm capable of being and he always stands by to make me what *I* want to be. Don loves the twenty-four-hour me, the lovable me, the flatulent me, the five-year-old me, the ballsy me, the quiet me (although he doesn't see *that* me too often), the angry me, the singer me, the sexy me, the business me, the menstrual me, the political me, the mischievous me...all of me. He likes the Frisbees I toss in his lap and tells me that with me, he will never be bored.

All I know is that I'm thankful his prior I do's didn't pan out. Now it's our turn—and I'm not going to give him back. The way I love my Don is bigger than all outer space.

EVIL LIVES IN AN EXHAUST FAN

I have had the pleasure of employing some different beings myself. *Carol's* was less than a mile from the bus station and just three blocks from the Justice Center. Many times, folks would come by after being released from jail and submit applications (asking to borrow a pen) when the ink hadn't dried on their walking papers yet. And for immediate help, I used to call the Drop Inn Center, a temporary shelter for homeless people that was located a few streets uptown. If the center didn't pan out, I was known to stand outside the restaurant and ask a few sidewalk-pacers if they wanted to put a decent meal in their stomach and make some cash for the day.

One of the first evening cooks' at *Carol's* was an older war veteran. He received government assistance because he had mental disorders; he sweat like a pig in a sauna and shook like a vibrating bed—but he could make one hell of a pot of chili! I instructed him to garnish all the plates coming out of the kitchen with a piece of lettuce and a slice of tomato—just something to add color. When I picked up a basket of potato chips I had ordered and found the basket fully lined with green leaf lettuce, how could I dare complain? After all, I had told him to garnish *everything* and besides, the man was so proud of his artistic ability.

Sometime after this artist, a gentleman from the Drop Inn Center was in my employ for about two months. He was probably the fifteenth cook I'd hired in a business that had been in an operation only two years. A nice, clean-cut fellow, sort of military looking, but I knew he was too good to be true. He worked out great in the beginning. After that, he quickly went downhill. It ended when I got a frantic phone call from him at six o'clock one Monday morning. "Carol, I can't come to work anymore!" he hollered. "I'm crazy, *CRAZY, CRAZY, CRAZY!*" Although his excuse was probably close to the truth, I would have done almost anything so I wouldn't have to work in the kitchen myself. "Okay, so you're crazy. But can't you at least make it through lunch?" I barked back. Didn't work.

Although I never saw him again, David Wilson ran into him at a bar several months later. The crazy man explained that it wasn't the pressures of being a short-order cook that made him quit, but something more supernatural. He told David that an evil energy lived in the exhaust fan in our kitchen, and that whatever it was had made his head spin completely around…twice. He also told David that I saw it happen. Now knowing me as you do, do you think I would remain on the q.t. about my cook doing a Linda Blair imitation? Can you imagine the publicity I could have gotten out of that one! It would have been twice as good as the visions of the Virgin Mary on the side of that barn in Conyers, Georgia.

But here's the real reason he left. He stole a thousand dollars out of the safe that I'd stupidly left open. I hadn't put two and two together until after he called in crazy. That was a ton of money for *Carol's* to lose. Three weekdays' revenues lost, and my payroll was due. When I was sure he was the thief, I called the Drop Inn Center to tell them my suspicions and was told that he'd packed his belongings and left just a few hours before. He never called for his paycheck. I guess he didn't need it.

After the human-dreidel, I hired a cook who was also an organic farmer. An excellent cook and very ingenious, his ingenuity sprouted in all levels. I found an apple-bong hidden in the tiny kitchen. He'd taken an apple and semi-cored it,

leaving an inch base at the bottom. Then he ad-libbed a screen
to hold the pot by puncturing pinholes in tin foil and then
shoved a straw in the fruit to draw out the smoke. Brilliant,
except for the fact that it was good for only two days before it
rotted. The clever cook and I had a nice little discussion.

There were four cases of wine in the basement that Fred
had bought at auction. I hadn't used any because all the bottles
had turned bad. I should have thrown them away—but Mac
took care of that for me. Mac came from the Drop Inn Center,
too, and I paid him $10 a day to clean *Carol's*. After letting him
go for a more dependable cleaning person, I found the empty
bottles of rank wine shoved into the ceiling rafters of the basement. Mac had received working benefits I'd not been aware
of. He was a terrible cleaner and kvetched constantly, but now
I know why he showed up every day.

FEELING STRONGER EVERY DAY

"What about a lease?" I asked Fred when I bought the business from him in 1990. "Nah, there was never a lease in the
thirty years this was *Chesnuts*," he replied. "Just mail Henry
the check the first of the month." He was referring to the
owner of the property and thus my new landlord. Henry had
been buddies with Fred's dad for nearly four decades and the
lease was "signed" with a friendly handshake.

After a year and a half of business at 811 Main Street,
Henry decided to open his own deli in his building (glad to
have fixed it for him). He gave me eighteen months to look for
another place where the new *Carol's Corner* would live and
prosper. Being banished from the property was a little jolt, to
say the least. For several weeks, however, I'd sensed that a big

change was lurking just around the corner. When Henry came in to tell me I was moving, I knew what he was going to say before the words came out of his mouth.

Being ousted was the best thing for the business. Henry had actually done me a favor since I'd always let people nudge me into taking action. Nothing more could be done at *Carol's* in that harbor. In stretching her arms, *Carol's* had outgrown her port. But it was frightening moving a business. I was afraid to move too far, because I might lose my clientele. But where was I going to find another place with the same feel that people loved? Would I be able to recapture the atmosphere?

It was about this time in 1992 that I met Don and the two of us fell in love. During the months of our courtship, a psychotic Fred started tightening his jealous grasp around my neck. He even demanded Don and I sign a prenuptial agreement, saying that Don would use me and go after my business. I thought that was preposterous and wouldn't even give it a thought. I was proud that I didn't bend to his controlling notions, considering my lifelong history as a human paper clip. Two years into a successful business, I was stronger and more sure of myself and my actions, and that gave him less power.

I believe Fred was feeling betrayed. I was spending more time with Don and less at the restaurant. Hey, I had a new life outside the joint. Fred didn't like that either. Because I was the owner of a popular hot spot, I was always being invited to social gatherings and charity functions and Fred had been my usual my escort. Not anymore. My fiancé Don was my date for these celebrations now.

I'm certain Fred felt threatened as well. Don was a businessman and owned his own heating and air conditioning contracting company and therefore knew about construction. I amassed strength from Don's knowledge and from his love. I listened to his ideas and construction advice and to his criticisms. Fred was gay but treated me as if he were a possessive, controlling husband. He was losing his hold on me and was running scared. No longer susceptible to his manipulation, I was only pacifying him because the liquor license had been transferred out of *Lee Chesnuts' Hideaway* into Fred's name—one step closer to being transferred into my name.

I still played it safe because Fred knew every facet of the business practices and made it clear in his own devious ways that if he had to, he would use anything against me. And I knew he would after the tricks he pulled, such as hiding my wallet and blaming it on a cook he didn't like so I would fire him for stealing. I was foggy as to exactly what had been done, but I feared that Fred may have altered the legal documents concerning the power of attorney that left *Lee Chesnuts* to him. That alone could stop the license from being transferred.

With a real estate agent and Fred's assistance, a new home was found for *Carol's*. It was a four-story building, constructed around 1900 and was only two doors up the street from *Carol's Corner*. The space had been vacant for seven years and the lease had no "friendship" ties. However, there was no heating or air conditioning or ventilation, and there was little electricity and even less plumbing. What did exist wasn't up to building codes. Small hurdles, right? Where was that five-gallon pickle bucket now? This time I needed financial institution loans. All the people I knew put together didn't have the type of money to lend to get the new *Carol's* built. An excellent customer, good friend, and an architect, Don Beck wanted to design the inside of the new place. Plus, his man of twenty years, Larry Eynon, volunteered to help in any capacity. Two humans for the price of one!

At the second anniversary party for the joint, everyone knew *Carol's* was on the move, but hadn't a clue as to where. We planned to take everyone in attendance outside and present them the proposed new space. It was too easy to walk twenty feet north to show them the site, so we devised a plan. We handed out pots, pans, and metal spoons as David, Greg, and I lined up the seventy-five or so people and led them on a parade around a few blocks with the kitchen percussion section clanking and banging away.

When we reached our destination everyone was invited into the dimly lit vacant building. We'd pasted plastic letters on the walls and floors spelling out words like *bar*, *restrooms*, and *kitchen* where these things would be built. Mom even flew in for the party. I'll never forget how proud she looked as I stood on a milk crate and recited a toast while everyone held up plastic champagne flutes and cheered with me. That night, dozens of people gave me their phone numbers and told me to call when the time came to paint, clean, tear down, or run errands. They wanted to help build their new home.

Play It Again, Sam

For Anthony "Tile Man" Clemons, who built this new home.

How many times do I have to heave myself into a blazing fire before I learn I'll be burnt to a crisp? My dad always said, "Screw me once, screw you! Screw me twice, screw me!" Words of wisdom. Fred postponed his move to Boston again, and this time I wasn't trying to shove him out the door, I was holding him. Things were tense and schitzy between us, but I needed him there for whatever he *could* do, because now we were starting from scratch and not just remodeling. True, I had Don. Although his company A & B Heating & Air Conditioning (gotta get a plug in there somewhere!) did a lot of the work and he gave more to me than advice and price breaks throughout this phase, he had his own enterprise to run. Fred drew the initial engineering plans needed so companies could bid their services. Sadly, I must admit that I was almost as clueless this round as in the first.

Although I had a business, I had very little capital; certainly far from the $200,000 or more needed to build and buy. So I applied for a loan from the city in April 1993. Before I locked it in through the Economic Department of Development, construction (which started months late again) was well into its third week. My name was the only one on all the signed-in-blood construction contracts and loan papers. *Carol's Corner* had borrowed $125,000 payable in five years with a low interest rate. How nerve-wracking it was when I thought that less than three years before, I'd gotten my first checkbook. Now here I was borrowing what weighed in my mind as a billion bucks in addition to the money I'd also borrowed from friends and family.

Included in the budget was the completion of the second floor where I would have my own cabaret room where I could sing. I wanted that room more than anything, but I could tell by this point in the construction that it wasn't financially feasible. With the time constraints tightening around me and the loan money dwindling before my eyes, I stopped all the construction on the second floor. Fred was irate with me for doing that and for the first time, I screamed back at him. No passive aggressive behavior on my part for a change. I let him know that this was *my* loan and that his simple and supposedly inexpensive ways had cost me more money in the long run. He was so surprised at my eruption that he didn't yell back.

A week before the new café opened, I closed the doors to the old one. How barren she looked inside as furnishings and equipment had been ripped away from her and placed in the new property. I felt so bad. It was as though she were the neglected older child after the new baby had been born. I swear, I could almost hear her walls crying.

The Board of Liquor Control agents from the state capital came for their final inspection on the Friday prior to *Carol's* opening on Monday. Everything passed except for one thing. The agents said they couldn't return to Cincinnati for at least a week and without their signatures, I couldn't open. I started to cry and told them the invitations had been mailed and hundreds of people would be here for the opening. What had not passed was the exposed plumbing pipes in the ceiling of the kitchen. The lady agent took tissues out of her purse and blotted my gushing tears.

The Universe was with me again on this one. My friend Larry Eynon was up on some scaffolding, painting a teal border around the lip of the ceiling where the purple (purple for healing) walls met. He looked down and recognized the tear-blotter from college. They ended up reminiscing and laughing and with that tie, the inspectors told us to have the drop ceiling installed by Monday. They said they would return early afternoon and we would pass inspection for the license to be transferred to my name (finally) and approved on opening day. Don was able to get a buddy of his to work a very long weekend so that *Carol's* could have a drop ceiling in the kitchen.

The transfer of the liquor license into my name was made final at 4:45 p.m. on June 21, 1993. The new doors opened at

5:00 p.m. For three years, I'd waited for this moment and here it was. This pink document was like a platinum brick in my hand. David Wilson knew about the soap-opera problems I'd been through with Fred, and he and I clasped hands in the middle of my new dining room on the wooden floor I had varnished fourteen hours earlier and jumped and screamed like children out of school for the summer.

I never could figure out why Fred finally put the license in my name. It didn't really matter. All I knew was that I no longer had to placate him. All I had to do now was to get rid of him as gently as possible. Don't get me wrong, I was not without feelings for Fred. I cared for him, felt his loneliness, and was sad for him for thinking he had to lavish money on people to get them to pretend to be his friends. I still felt some sense of gratitude for his having presented me with the opportunity to buy a restaurant. At the same time, I was a bit angry with myself because it's unspiritual to string a human being along, even though I knew he'd been playing me from the start.

Fred didn't have a job. He didn't have to have one. He lived nicely on the $500 per week salary that I'd paid him since October 1990 and had continued to pay him for nearly three years. He also frequently used a corporate American Express card from *Carol's* for travel, clothes, and other inspirations. He bought presents for family, friends, and me with my own credit card. The man threw a $2,500 party for his parents' fiftieth wedding anniversary at my place and *Carol's* picked up the tab, and he brought countless friends and family members to eat and drink free of charge. He'd been living off my business, but now he'd have to look in the classifieds to find another premium sucker. I was through playing the part.

BE CAREFUL WHAT YOU WISH FOR

In keeping with the original *Carol's* at 811 Main Street, the new *Carol's* at 825 Main opened on the same birthday, Summer Solstice, June 21, 1993. Although *Carol's* wasn't on the corner anymore, changing the name wasn't even an issue. Why fix the one thing that ain't broke?

Fred left for Boston an hour into the grand opening party and I was ecstatic. However, opening day was purified chaos as it is for any business. Cheap champagne flowed freely and as I looked around at all these strangers in my new restaurant, I felt like an inanimate object completely removed from my own creation. Customers propped open the beautiful new windows so people could climb in and out and hand libations to any passerby on the sidewalk — dangerous *and* illegal. Many of these people were not my regular customers I'd known and loved for years, and I had no idea where the new people were coming from. Don Beck and Larry came over to me as I sat in the corner as full of life as a cadaver. They suggested and helped me close and lock all the windows — I wasn't competent enough to devise that plan by myself.

My brain had runneth over and I literally ceased to function. I felt as barren inside as my old place looked now. I was unable to glide around and shake hands. Fortunately, my manager David Wilson and assistant manager Greg and the additional staff I hired had it on the ball. They made stations and came up with their own abbreviations to write on guest checks to get food and drinks. They pulled themselves together and handled the huge drinking crowd. Before the grand opening, I wasn't able to concern myself with comprising the daily mechanics of service in the restaurant because I spent too much time putting out fires and was so involved in hands-on building the damn thing. I simply ran out of time and mental energy.

Then unfolded a revolting casualty. With the umpteenth flush of a new john, the basement floor drains started to burp up raw sewage and all the sludge backed into the drainage hoses for the three walk-in refrigerators. I learned during my frantic late night call to the plumber that this could have been avoided if we'd installed a new trunk line as he'd recommended. At the time, however, Fred hadn't seen the need for the $700 expense which was about one-half the cost of this emergency repair job. (This problem continued for nearly five years.)

After the poop explosion excitement died down, the merriment for the champagne crowd resumed. I took this opportunity to walk back to my apartment and change my clothes from sparkle to jeans. On the way back, I sat on the curb by my old place and wailed to myself. I missed her already. In fact, I missed her before I left her. I told myself I didn't like the new space and that I'd never get used to it. It's just too big for me, I moaned into the night air. Don found me outside in tears and gently handed me over to Mom and told her to put me to bed. The party hadn't more than an hour to go and he stayed around and helped my employees clean up afterwards. In between, he fried burgers because the cooks I'd hired weren't trained and couldn't get anything—cooked or raw—out of the kitchen.

Over the next few days, I gradually slipped back into owner mode and hired and fired, revised, rescheduled, rearranged, and bought machines and equipment. After a week or two of business in my new place, I followed Don's advice and sought an attorney to get rid of Fred. He told me to stop paying him immediately. I couldn't wait to get him out of my life and business, but I knew it would crush him and make him angrier.

Carol's had been open for several weeks when Fred returned from Boston where he'd been looking for a house. When he came by, he said he wanted his latest paycheck and also told me I needed to pay him for the weeks he was in the East. I refused to pay him anymore and told him that I wasn't going to play his game any longer. He was calm, but his face turned scarlet as he told me that we were business partners and that if I didn't want him around anymore, I could buy him out of his half of the business for $180,000. He said that the contract I'd signed three years prior and had tucked away in a secret compartment proved it.

Signed contract? Business partner? How could we be business partners? It was my name on the lease, my name on the loans, my name on the door. I asked him how we could be partners when the corporate papers that were filed over three years ago had my name and my name only on every document. I was president, vice president, secretary, and treasurer of my corporation. I owned 100 shares of stock in this corporation called *Carol's Corner Café*. In fact, from the get-go, he told me never to call him or introduce him as a partner, because he didn't want anyone thinking that he was. When I reminded him of these facts, he said everything was put in my name in order to avoid any entanglements with his previous businesses. Fred and me partners?

Fred, who knew that Don and I were to be married in about six weeks, threatened to stop our marriage. I don't even know why he wanted to do that or how he could. Right before he left, I told him that he wasn't welcome in my restaurant anymore, and the last thing I heard from him was, "I'll see you in court!" And I knew he would.

WE JUST WANNA SAY "WE DO!"

All Don and I wanted to do was get married. We had both been through hell opening *Carol's* and we didn't want a big, showy to-do, or even a small one for that matter. We explained to our families and friends that the past few months of building and opening a restaurant had pulverized our nerves. We just wanted to wed and go on a relaxing honeymoon.

It didn't matter to me whether a judge married us, but Don wanted a person of some kind of cloth to administer our vows. Don is Catholic and I'm Jewish, so there weren't many choices in the matter, but Rabbi Sol Greenberg was perfect for our needs. He was the only clergyperson in Cincinnati who would perform what most religious leaders call a *mixed* marriage. When I learned that fact, I felt like I was marrying a non-mammal.

The ceremony was held on August 13 and included only Don, his daughter Amy, the Rabbi, a photographer, and me, and still it did have all the elements of a traditional wedding. For something old, I wore my grandma's pearls; for something new, an eggshell colored pantsuit that my mother bought me; for something borrowed, I carried Paula's handkerchief; for something blue, I wore a sassy blue garter on my thigh.

Amy was the sweetest combination little flower girl, maid of honor, bridesmaid, groomsman, usher, and best man. She and I carried bouquets of calla lilies and Don wore a single, white rose boutonniere. Don and I sipped Manischewitz Concord Grape wine from my parents' silver Kiddish cup (a Jewish wine goblet which is a tradition symbolic of the "sharing of common destiny"). We weren't married under a chupah, (canopy) but Don did break a drinking glass wrapped in a cloth napkin, while Rabbi Greenberg shouted Mazeltov and kissed the three of us. I think he even kissed the photographer.

Returning from our honeymoon towards the third week of August, I was happy to find that my managers had kept the place together and running smoothly. But oh god, the work I had ahead of me! I was working in the kitchen during lunch when a uniformed police officer came to see me. He was there to serve me papers. I was now referred not only as Mrs. Sherman-Jones, but also as the Defendant.

Intermission

THAT'S A BUNCH OF GARBAGE!

The first *Carol's* generated tons of garbage—too much, in fact, for the biweekly city-run sanitation department to dispose of properly. I needed trash collection every day, but it was too expensive to rent a dumpster and have a private trash company collect. This is when I learned to barter. I struck a deal with the orange-overalled city workers one-on-one.

To have the trash picked up daily required some personal compensation. In a paper bag placed next to the garbage cans was a cold six-pack of Old Milwaukee waiting for these gentlemen. Even though I didn't carry that taste on my beverage menu, I ordered it especially for them. After two weeks of this new system, however, we ran into a snag. The driver dude came in to have a serious private discussion with me. He informed me that if I didn't get a more sophisticated brand of suds, they would no longer be coming daily. They petitioned a more provocative taste and recommended Colt 45 Malt Liquor or Pabst Blue Ribbon. I easily obliged their demands and from that moment on, there was no rubbish between us.

BOO AND MRS. HOWELL

On Halloween 1991, we turned *Carol's Corner* into *Gilligan's Island*. We had nets with plastic fish hung on the walls, served a Shipwreck Punch, fish sticks, and Mary Ann's coconut pies for hors d'oeuvres. My buddy John even dressed up like an island girl, with a coconut bra and a palm frond hula skirt. I was Ginger, David Wilson was Gilligan, Greg was the pilot Wrongway Feldman, my waitress Andrea was Mary Ann, my cook Marty was the Skipper, and my friend Boo was Mrs. Howell.

Boo was perfect for the role. Never mind that he is six-foot four, thin, and has a receding hairline. Trust me. He made a *great* Mrs. Howell in his makeup and wig. He wore a 1960s, pastel, mohair skirt-suit and modest pumps, and his lace-gloved hands carried a pocketbook containing a compact and lipstick that he kept taking out for touchups. Boo could have been cloned from Mrs. Howell's DNA. The only thing odd was watching "Lovey" smoke a cigarette.

Boo sat at the bar for most of the party, delicately sipping on cocktails. But shortly after midnight, he left to go kick up his heels at The Dock (the gay dance bar where I'd once sent that obnoxious Shriner) where he met his Mr. Howell for the evening. When Boo woke up in Mr. Howell's apartment in the morning, he realized all he had to wear was his Mrs. Howell costume. And to top that off, the only way home for him was on foot. Walking home the morning after an interlude is what David Wilson calls the "walk of shame." Poor Boo. It was morning rush hour traffic as Mrs. Howell made his way home. Did he wear the whole shebang—wig, makeup, suit, hose, gloves and pumps—for his stride home? "Well, of *course*, I did!" he said, astonished that I'd felt the need to ask. "I would have looked silly if I hadn't!"

VALOR IS AN APHRODISIAC

I'd struck a deal with the owners of the parking lot across the street from the restaurant so my customers and employees could get a break from paying full price. Still, almost every evening, the cars were broken into and vandalized. At phone stations around *Carol's*, we posted the number to file a police report so we could at least be somewhat accommodating to our shattered guests. But it was ridiculous. This turned some folks against coming downtown to party. I should have given out coupons for car-window repair with every meal purchased. It turned out that the lot-lords were also tow-fiends who had trucks waiting to haul when a forgetful patron didn't slip a buck into the metal box used when the attendant wasn't on duty. When a demon truck scoped the lot, guest or worker would scream "Tow truck!" and the absentminded would abruptly file out the door and hustle across to the silver slotted box.

One time, Don and his manager Greg List came down to *Carol's* during a Friday happy hour. Greg's car got hooked and I instantly knew that he was a culpable forgetter. I ran out to stop the dude from towing the car. I knew the gig of paying twenty-five bucks for a "drop fee" to free the vehicle and all that I needed was to run across to the cash register and grab some dough. But the driver-scum said a few choice words and shouted that he wasn't going to unhook the car. He was determined to tow it. So I stood in front of his truck with my foot propped up on the bumper in my Maggie London crepe, split-up-to-my-neck black dress and refused to budge.

Within a flash, my husband came out from the restaurant and tried to reason with the hyper-tensed repo-man. Don had cash in his hand but the Neanderthal wouldn't take it. He shoved his greasy finger in Don's face and yelled, "You! You get your bitch outta the way!" Don lost it. In a total William Holden kind of manner, he threw his custom-made jacket to the pavement and gestured for the jerk to get out of his truck. "Come on! Come over here! Come on!" he shouted. The entire restaurant was now emptied onto the parking lot and one by one, they circled the truck like a wagon train during an ambush. Although Don's manager tried to calm him down, we were surrounded by forty-eight highly enflamed queens who intensified the dispute by yelling to my husband, "Get him, Tiger! Get him!" A few of the boys even formed a cheerleading line. All they lacked were pom-poms. The driver remained frozen in the cab of his truck. He probably couldn't figure out whether he was going to get his hair and nails done or have the internal organs beaten out of him. Although my raised leg on the bumper was beginning to tingle with numbness, I was not about to leave my post.

Two cop cars pulled up because they had heard the revolt from down the street. They made the pinhead take the drop fee and leave the car. Someone called *The Cincinnati Enquirer* and the story appeared in the paper the following week. I got a ton of free publicity. And how 'bout that man of mine defending my honor! Ain't he somethin'? I'll tell you a secret...I couldn't wait to get home that night. As I rushed to be in the arms of my hero, I realized that for me—the *valoree*—that valor was quite an aphrodisiac. I soon discovered, however, that it can also put the *valorer* into a sound slumber.

SAVING DAD

He would have been the last person on Earth I thought would save a human being's life. "Crystal," was cute and peppy, with a deafening speaking voice and in school studying to be the next Pavarotti. He had big, blue, puppy-innocent eyes, perfectly straight, white teeth, a steady smile, flushed cheeks, and ash blond hair. He looked like a wholesome farm boy without muscles. Crystal was an apt server, sweet but very ditzy.

Crystal was waiting on a table of thirteen who were celebrating a family member's college graduation. Everyone was busy eating, drinking, and chatting when Crystal noticed the man at the head of the table—the dad of the brood—had slumped over in his chair and was turning blue. Immediately, Crystal pressed into action. He calmly put down his serving tray, and knelt down by dad. "Sir...are you choking?" he asked gently. Dad, who couldn't speak, just nodded. With that, Crystal powerhoused dad to his feet, stood behind him with his chest pressed against the man's back, wrapped his arms around the man's chest, clasped his hands, and performed the Heimlich maneuver. The larynx-lodged food projected and spiraled clear across the party table. Crystal was a hero.

The family was awestruck by the quick thinking of this young man and couldn't thank him enough. When they left the restaurant, however, they appreciated Crystal with a measly eight percent gratuity. Perhaps before Crystal saved good ol' dad, he should have asked the family if it would affect his tip.

OPEN MOUTH, INSERT CHEESECAKE

I had come downstairs from my office on the second floor to reward myself with a lemonade after doing a bushel of paperwork. The restaurant was at a mid-afternoon lull and I sat at the bar and chatted with a patron. He asked me if I had seen the musical *Grease* that was playing at the Aronoff Center. I said no, but I didn't stop there. I went on to say how Sally Struthers, one of the leads in the touring production, had gotten so fat. I'd seen how she'd blimped-up in the TV commercials where she soulfully begged to the American public to sponsor a starving child. And *then* I had to add how she must sample all the food designated for those poor urchins. I chuckled at my own enormously creative wit, while my bartender stood wide-eyed and horrified. She then whispered, "Sally's in the restaurant having a late lunch." I burnt with embarrassment. My body went limp. I was sure she had heard me. The jukebox wasn't playing and after I finished punishing myself by repeatedly thwacking my head on the edge of the bar, I slowly eyed the restaurant. There she was, sitting quietly with some friends at the only occupied table in the joint.

What to do? What to do? Do I say something? How did I dare apologize for my tremendous faux pas? Do I tell her how much I loved her on *All In The Family*? Tell her what a great thing she was doing for such a noble charity? How could I redeem myself?

I sent her table a plate full of cheesecake and ran upstairs to hide.

THE NIGHT THE DRAG QUEEN FELL ON MY HUSBAND

Before Don and I hooked up, he knew gay people. I, however, put the glaze on the donut.

He and I were at The Dock. *Carol's* had bought a table for a Drag Christmas Benefit and we were watching Pissonya Peoples perform "I Saw Mommy Kissing Santa Claus," when the poor thing fell off her heels, toppled from the stage into my husband's lap, and then finished the fall to the floor. Leave it to a drag queen for all that drama. Mind you, Pissonya was far from petite. She knocked the wind out of my man's sails. But Don, proving chivalry is not dead, reached for the wounded Pissonya and helped her to her feet. Hurt, bewildered, and out of character, Pissonya gave Don a big macho pat on the butt and in a low man-voice said, "Thanks, Don." Don didn't know what to else to say but, "No problem, man," as he stood there and watched Pissonya hobble backstage.

As we settled back in our seats after the floor show, Don asked me how the drag queen knew his name and said he thought he recognized the voice. I informed my husband that the drag queen who fell into his lap was one of the waiters at a restaurant we frequented. Always amazing me, he replied, "Really? I didn't know he could sing!"

NORMAL CAN BE PEEING AT A URINAL NEXT TO A MAN WEARING A PINK SEQUINED GOWN

Glitter, sequins, mall-hair, no hair, spiked hair, expensive diamonds, nose rings, cheap jewelry, leather, spandex, cashmere, jeans, glamour, and tattoos. Just another Friday evening at *Carol's Corner Café*, a place where we learned to expect the unexpected and assume the unassumable. We never knew what would fly into the restaurant or vogue out of the closet.

Several conventions were in town. Among them were the Pipefitters Union and also Tri-ESS/The Society for the Second Self (a national organization of heterosexual male transvestites). A group of each came into *Carol's* on this momentous eve.

The lights in *Carol's* were always dim in the evening and the music at a low roar—it could be Aerosmith or Ella Fitzgerald, the jukebox was as diverse as the clientele. Several large, flannel-and-T-shirt-clad pipefitters were at a table peacefully waiting on their pound o' beef and fried carbohydrates. At another table a few feet away—but worlds apart—were a dozen gigantic K-Mart-prom-dressed, heavily foundationed, cross-dressers, daintily sipping on Pink Ladies, Sidecars, and Manhattans, trying to remember to keep their legs crossed and pinkies extended. No scarce amount of light could fool anyone's 20/20 into believing these broads were born females. Most of these chicks were almost as tall as Michael Jordan and wore more face paint than Sitting Bull at war.

It was just a matter of time.
I could hear the bomb ticking.
I was prepared for battle.

And just as sure as the hair on those girls' knuckles, the first verbal catapult hurled through the dining room. One of the good ol' boys busted out with, "Hey! Look at all them big faggots in dresses over there!" The icing on the cake? The jukebox was between songs.

I launched into action. I walked over to the Budweiser-bottle-studded table, introduced myself as the owner, and nicely, but matter-of-factly informed these men that *Carol's* was a place for everybody. It was a place for everyone to feel welcome, including themselves, and language such as that was not tolerated in this house. If they had a problem with that, they could pay their bill and leave.

It

    was

        that

            simple.

As I was calmly administering the only warning the union boys would receive, one of the big-boned, cross-dressing gals put his hand on my shoulder. He told me he could speak their language and strongly suggested I move aside. His request was, to say the least, unusual. Either the managers of *Carol's* or I normally mediated this type of situation. With some hesitation, I backed away from the table and listened.

The first move he made was to buy them a beer and a shot. Then he opened his purse, took out his wallet (as he did, one of his nails peeled off into a basket of potato chips) and showed them a photo of a pretty woman—his wife. He explained that he was not gay and then threw the topic of transvestitism out on the table. "Ask me and my friends any questions you may have," he encouraged the pipefitters, "and we'll answer them as honestly as we can."

I thought he would be chewed up and spit out. I saw him as multicolored-mincemeat and couldn't believe anyone would be so bold and fearless as to purposely set themselves up for a battering showdown. At best, I expected verbal warfare between tables 21 and 22. But phooey on me. What did I know?

A few pipefitters started asking legitimate questions.

In a New York second, most of the unioners sprung from the table. It was beyond their vision, something they couldn't grasp and didn't want to know anything about. They probably weren't as secure with themselves as the ones who remained. But the others were sincerely intrigued and interested. They were up for learning something about a culture of which they were ignorant. No raised voices or cheap shots. No machismo-antagonistic play. Plus, when the food arrived, some extras were given to the men in dresses by the men in T-shirts. The worlds apart shook hands.

Tiny baby steps is what it takes to change the world, and Ms. Tri-ESS—he was on it.

This was exactly why *Carol's* was. It was why the Universe worked so hard with me to get this restaurant together. I believe *Carol's* was designed to fulfill a purpose, to bring the Earth's people a little closer together. When building this place, I cemented a huge piece of amethyst into the tile above the front door entrance. This crystal's metaphysical makeup is known to help open the third eye in people so they wouldn't be so narrow-minded. If we're ever to unite this world of ours, we've got to start in our own backyard.

Don told me that before I introduced him to these people, he had viewed the cross-dressing scene as abnormal. After hanging at *Carol's* for a spell, however, he learned that "normal" can be peeing at a urinal next to a man wearing a pink sequined gown.

Ignorance is not bliss.

It should be abolished.

THE DEL-RAES

This story is dedicated to Jeff "Bambi" Boss who died from AIDS-related complications at thirty-three years young in 1996.

I met the Del-Raes through Bambi (a nickname given him because of his huge, tranquil, brown eyes), the gentleman who owned a small cleaning company that I had contracted with to clean my restaurant. Bambi's boyfriend at the time, Lenny, was a member of "The Del-Rae Sisters" who performed at functions and gay clubs around town, lip-synching their way through songs from the forties. They each had faux first names designed to sound fancy. There was Maggie Magnolia Del-Rae, Billina Del-Rae, and Bodena Del-Rae.

It was high noon at *Carol's Corner Café* and patrons were lined up out into the street waiting to be seated to purchase the $3.99 meat loaf and mashed potato special. Lunch is a race against the clock. The dining room fills up quickly with work-serious customers who have only a short time to walk to the restaurant, order, eat, pay, tip (sometimes they apparently didn't have enough time to tip), and rush back to their offices. My jobs at lunch were to gather a list of those who wished to dine, help run food out of the kitchen, answer the phone for to-go orders, and clean the tables quickly so we could turn them as many times as possible.

I was always honest with people when I took their names for a table, knowing they had only half an hour or so to spare. If it took five minutes to be seated, that's what I told them. If it was going to be half an hour, I told them that, too. If they chose to wait, most of them would watch each and every step I took, staring at me with some hostility and annoyed that I was unable to pull a table with six chairs out of my navel.

We were in the middle of one of the busiest lunches when the Del-Raes showed up in full drag to pay me a tribute. You would think an army of police officers had entered the restaurant from the awed stillness that gripped the lunchtime masses. And the funny thing was that time seemed to slow down as soon as the gals strolled into the room. They found me crouched down in the center of the dining room scraping a stepped-on french fry off of the floor. Like Prince Charming to Cinderella, Maggie Magnolia offered his hand and helped me to my feet. The Del-Raes wanted to thank me on behalf of the gay community for the charitable works my restaurant had done. Then they proceeded to crown me as an "Honorary Del-Rae Sister" right there on the spot.

Singing and dancing to a 1940s swing tune, they conferred upon me the name of "Grillita Fromage Del-Rae" (which, I am honored to say, means Grilled Cheese Del-Rae). After my coronation, the acclaimed Del-Raes announced who they were and the high rank they had just bestowed upon me. Then sister Maggie proclaimed in his North Carolinian drawl, "Please…*every*one…take those forks out of your mouths, get your derrières off those chairs, and rise to help us applaud this woman!" This was a tremendous honor, you know, being that I'm the only Del-Rae Sister born without a scrotum.

The previously highly-tensed lunch crowd did just what Maggie told them to do and, after a stirring round of applause, fellow sisters and guests chanted at the tops of their lungs in their suits (or padded brassieres), "Speech! Speech!"

Years after that momentous event, the crowd who had participated in my crowning had a different tone about them. Perhaps it's because with the Sisters' encouragement, they had laughed and engaged in some fun to fit into their hectic work schedules. Every time a guest who was present during that ceremonial day brought someone into *Carol's* who wasn't aware of my queenship, I was always asked to come over to be introduced as Grillita Fromage Del-Rae, and only then as the owner of the establishment. When I left the table, I heard giggles and carrying on about that celebratory escapade. People were glad to be a part of it. Sometimes, you just gotta stop and smell the cheeses.

ACT II
The Show

You Build, We'll Supply

Our first round of T-shirts affirmed our new logo: *Carol's Corner Café...Just The Same, But Better!* And it was better. Better for the Cincinnati Tax Revenue Department, for the Ohio Sales Tax Division, for the Bureau of Workers Compensation, for the city's employment ratio, for Fifth Third Bank, for Central Trust, for the Internal Revenue Service, for the Hamilton County Tax Commission, and for the lawyer who was defending me against Fred.

At the old place, I had been responsible for the livelihood of seven people, but the new joint was so much bigger that I fired that many people in the first week! By the end of 1993, around forty people were employed by *Carol's Corner Café*, Inc., and most of them were full-time. The new *Carol's* had an occupancy of one hundred and thirty-nine people, nearly three times the number of the old *Carol's*. And though many thankless entities benefited from *Carol's* expansion, it could have been worse, of course. I could have been lamenting over ways of getting folks in the door. But the Universe had me in her plans: You build, we'll supply.

Carol's quickly became the place to be seen. Casts and crews from productions at the nearby Aronoff Center for the Arts, a brand new, eighty-two million dollar theatre complex, spent their time off refreshing themselves at our place. The crowds continued to grow. The atmosphere worked.

All I really wanted to do, however, was bartend like I did four nights a week at the little place, where I could see every person walk in and yell lovingly (and sometimes truthfully) as they exited, "Thanks for leaving!" However, I didn't tend bar at the new place. I couldn't. I needed to be out in front seating, schmoozing (which I liked), or rectifying a bad situation (which I didn't like). I needed free hands to mop up sewage-skank in the basement (that continued to belch up every six months or so) or to plunge and clean the puke of overindulgent customers (that continued…well, forever). For cryin' out loud, I was the owner! I would never ask people to do things I wouldn't do myself. As a result, I hadn't a moment to spend with my beloved old customer friends, nor anywhere near enough time to spend time with my new husband and step-daughter. Fortunately, I didn't have to see my "business partner" any longer. Fred had finally moved to Boston.

I quickly realized that I didn't like the restaurant business at all. The bar, however, remained my first and true love. The first *Carol's* was a bar that offered a very small menu of basic food—hamburgers, sandwiches, french fries—if the cook came to work. The new *Carol's* was a restaurant with a bar. And though I'd had trouble keeping employees at the *Corner Café*, it was nothing like I experienced at the new place. Within the first six weeks in the new and improved *Carol's*, I had to fire the lead cook for stealing bottles of vodka.

Carol's brought in many theatregoers who longed for more than burgers and fries, so I replaced the lead cook with a chef whom I'd known through another eatery. But a broadened menu not only required a chef, but also a sous-chef, prepcooks and more dishwashers and more managers and more supervisors and more servers and more bartenders and barbacks and more janitors...and yikes! Somebody stop the madness!

I just wanted my little ten-foot by six-foot kitchen back where we used to clip food orders onto a piece of wire with clothespins. The same kitchen where Marty, a most rotund cook, burned the underside of his belly on the stove each time he turned around (it just made the burgers taste better). Marty was with me for two years before getting addicted to crack. Eventually, he got whacked out and left in the midst of a turbo-charged Saturday night...but boy, those were the days!

I was stubborn about getting classier food and I didn't want to stop serving the grease-drenched hamburgers that people loved or the basket of cheese fries that had been so popular for more than three years. My new chef agreed with not tossing the good ol' standbys, but he and David Wilson convinced me that there was a way *Carol's* could satisfy all palates. They were right.

It was exciting to acquire the reputation of owning a restaurant that offered a great menu with delicious specials daily and nightly, as well as burgers and fries. *Carol's* received fantastic reviews from *The Cincinnati Post*, *The Cincinnati Enquirer*, *Cincinnati Magazine*, and some other local publications. The reviewer from *Cincinnati Magazine* was especially delighted with *Carol's* character. Just as her table was to receive their meal, the plate-laden tray fell to the kitchen floor. David Wilson told the critic and her guests that there was an accident in the kitchen and their food would be just a little while longer. "Oh no!" the reviewer gasped. "An accident? I hope nobody was hurt!" "No," David assured her, "but you should have seen your chicken!" They *loved* David and when it finally arrived, they loved their chicken, too.

On a flight to Arizona, I paged through Delta Airline's *Sky* magazine and was astounded and proud to read a glowing article suggesting that city visitors dine and relax at *Carol's*. Also, David Wilson entered our new menu in a best-looking-menu contest sponsored by National Restaurant Association. My little joint in downtown Cincinnati came in second only to Steven Spielberg's Los Angeles restaurant called Splash!

WHAT GOES AROUND, COMES AROUND

For the first year or so, my first chef worked out great. Then his personality started to fester. He became temperamental, ornery, stubborn, and rude — but not to customers. In fact, our patrons respected him and loved the new food he brought in. Among the employees, however, he created a war and in the process, built a "Berlin Wall" between the front staff and the back staff. You don't have to be in the food business to know that many chefs have problem egos. His dislike for both David Wilson and me was apparent, and he ridiculed us to the other employees. There was no way I was going to let him ruin my place; I didn't care how good he was. When he ordered me out of "his" kitchen, I knew things would have to change. I started secretly interviewing other chefs to take over his position.

On a busy Friday night during this walking-on-eggshell time, one of the employees told me that some staff members were smoking pot in the kitchen and blowing the smoke into the exhaust system. I was livid. Not only was it illegal and dangerous, it could destroy my liquor license if we were busted. I lunged into the kitchen and demanded to know where the paraphernalia was and who was indulging. I called an emergency full-staff meeting for the next afternoon.

Not blaming one person or one group in particular, I spoke to all of them about the dangers of being high and working. I told my employees that I had been guilty of the same act at Rusconi's years ago and I understood how this could happen. I told them when you're young and don't own your own establishment, you don't think of the consequences. I stressed that no one would have a job without that small, pink permit. I didn't fire the one or two individuals who took part in the dope smoking because I knew they weren't the only outlaws. After the meeting, however, the chef took the kitchen staff out for a walk to talk before they had to prepare the evening specials. Not only did they talk, they passed around a joint while he mocked my lecture. Unfortunately, I didn't find out about it until weeks after the meeting.

I had a chef on hold while he tidied things up for his career move over to my place, but on the day in September 1995 that I learned of what had happened among the kitchen staff after my speech about drug use on the job, I fired him. When I told him I knew all about his walk-and-talk, he couldn't understand why I was so incensed. He said he didn't provide the joint nor did he smoke it, and that he could not control what people do on the outside of work. I reminded him that the employees had been clocked in for the meeting and I was paying them to get high on my time. He wasn't sorry and refused to see my point. That was it. He was gone. I called the chef-in-waiting right after he walked out the front door. Later that evening, when Chef Ken Schad came in for his first shift, the front-of-the-house and a few of the back-of-the-house staff gave him a round of applause.

While the circumstances and people varied, sickening situations like that always happened, sometimes as intense, sometimes not. I wanted to be friends with all my employees and I wanted to make everyone happy. I wanted everyone to like me and it wasn't possible, only taxing. I had to maintain some distance so I could keep an eye on all of them. I hated that and as a result, didn't do well with that aspect of the business at all.

A major problem in the restaurant business is stealing. I had definitely paid my karmic bill. I thought I knew all the angles but—besides the old steaks-wrapped-in-plastic-and-left-by-the-dumpster-to-pick-up-after-work trick—some new methods had been discovered since my slick finger days. One busboy walked out with two brand new chairs and about twenty CDs I'd brought from home. Even employees who don't label it stealing, steal. Many of them felt that if they picked up a shift when I was in dire need or helped decorate the place for whatever holiday on their own time, they and/or their friends deserved a piece of cake or a few extra cocktails. Years ago at The Bistro, I'd load my pockets full of Sweet'N Low for home use. And if I could get away without paying for lunch, I'd do it. I loved working there and was friends with the owners. I never considered that stealing but, of course, it was.

I think if saccharin was all that had disappeared from my joint, I wouldn't have had any complaints.

"You can't find good help like you used to" is an understatement. I did have some superior employees in both the front and the back of house, but the endless strength it took to continue hiring and firing was debilitating. Just when I thought I had a good staff, someone failed to show up, or four people put in notice at the same time, or someone stole and got caught, or someone wound up in prison, or someone came to work drunk or stoned, or one loud-spoken and disgruntled employee would rebel and gather other followers. I couldn't keep up. The new place was so big I didn't even know all my employees' astrological signs, for heaven's sakes!

CAROL'S WAS HER OWN SOAPBOX

"I just came out to my parents. They accept it, but they're scared for me. They only know the stereotype of a gay person: sexual promiscuity and loneliness in an isolated world. I brought them into *Carol's* to show them that I hang out just like anyone else in a place where I'm respected, where I have friends, and where I'm surrounded by all kinds of people. They felt much better. They even come in here without me to have fun on their own. *Carol's* helped alter their views. Thank you for having this place. You have no idea."

Gay parents also felt comfortable bringing in their children of all ages and I was thanked for that, too. If I had a dime for every time I was praised for opening *Carol's*, I'd be the wealthiest broad in the world. And each time I was praised, I was also humbled (believe it or not), because I felt I did little to deserve such thanks. I'm glad that I provided a safe place, an atmosphere where cultures fused, but that was all I provided. The real praise belonged to the people of strength unfolding *themselves* to their loved ones.

Carol's had a social conscience. Yes, she was me, but she breathed her own duty. It was as if *Carol's* were the central nervous system of the community. Beginning in 1990 with each death of a friend or customer from AIDS, *Carol's* sent a $50 donation to an AIDS charity. That continued for many years — way too many. Stonewall, a human rights organization, frequently came to *Carol's* for support and often set up information booths there where they handed out pamphlets designed to raise public awareness on basic human rights issues as well as gay issues. Whether Republican or Democrat, judges and folk running for city offices ate at *Carol's*. District One police officers were always there when we needed them. Off-duty cops came in with friends and family to eat and party. The art, symphony, and ballet communities also patronized *Carol's*. The Sharks Soccer Team, who won the gold medal in the 1994 Gay Olympics in New York, made *Carol's* their hub. PFLAG (Parents & Friends of Lesbians and Gays) came in to frolic after meetings. We lent space to the Cincinnati Men's Chorus for many of their benefit concerts and they made *Carol's* their stomping ground. We helped, the Freestore/Foodbank, AVOC (AIDS Volunteers of Cincinnati), F.A.C.E (For AIDS Children Everywhere), The Ryan White Foundation, the Ensemble Theater of Cincinnati, and centers for abused women, and the School for Creative & Performing Arts. One year, Rob and Steve set up a booth to register people to vote.

Perhaps I was subconsciously trying to redeem myself from my past wrongs or maybe it was the Universe's way of allowing me to repay bad karma. Who knows? Perhaps people and organizations came to us because there was no segregation between *Carol's* and the rest of the world. *Carol's* encompassed and embraced the world.

THE CHIEF SOIRÉE

This story is dedicated to Steve Grayson who performed in many of the benefits held at Carol's. Steve died in 1998 at the age of thirty-seven from AIDS-related complications.

In honor of my friend Ron, *Carol's* held "The Annual Ron Stephens Non-Celebrity Benefit" each year around holiday time. All the proceeds went to Caracole, a non-profit housing organization in Cincinnati for individuals and families living with HIV/AIDS. (Caracole's slogan is "It's About Living" and it's right on because this organization not only supplies housing, but it also teaches people how to *live* with AIDS.) The first year, our benefit brought Caracole House more than $600 and every year the sum grew larger. With the last benefit, *Carol's* handed close to $10,000 in cash to this much-needed charity. Within eight years, we'd raised over $54,000 for Caracole.

The benefits were delightful and warm, but the ebullient feeling of the audience and the participants was nearly indescribable. All involved gave so much of themselves. It was a time when people forgot about petty divisions and became one huge, breathing organism opening up to let more cells in. *Carol's* closed to the public on benefit night to squeeze in as many ticket buyers as possible. The night started with cocktails, then dinner, a raffle, and an upbeat and sometimes off-tempo show. Many AIDS benefits tend to be still and somber, but I wanted it to be fun and vivacious. I figured we all know why we are here, so let's celebrate life!

The dinner was donated by different food purveyors and restaurants, so *Carol's* wouldn't have to absorb all the costs. Other restaurants, live theatres, movie theatres, clothing stores, hair salons, and gift shops donated the prizes for the raffle. All we had to do was ask for things and companies both large and small gave. Sometimes, we wouldn't even have to ask! Employees gave their time to cook, serve, and clean up. If they were tipped, they gave their gratuities to Caracole. On the day of the event, friends and customers turned the restaurant into a theatre. The soundboard throughout these yearly shindigs was run by Jim McCormick and David Adams. I hadn't met Jim, but when he heard about the first benefit, he wanted to take part. Jim had known Ron through church. Then Jim galloped David into the picture. That is how it worked. Everyone banded together. The benefit not only generated money, but also a ton of love...and the love was paramount. To my knowledge, Ron's family never knew about these events.

Carol's was all of what Rob and Steve contrived in her birth chart and everything I asked for: fun, acceptance, change, love, harmony, and family. I know that one of the reasons *Carol's* was a success was because she always put back into the community more than she took.

THAT'S NOT ENTERTAINMENT

Carol's was a beautiful place—a superb example of restoration and revitalization in an oppressed and neglected downtown. The location was in a prime area—only a block or so from the Aronoff Center and right next to a crack house.

Not all the tenants in the apartment building next to *Carol's* were drug addicts, prostitutes, dealers, and pimps, but most were. Pimps would scream and beat up on their girls right in front of *Carol's*. This is not the type of happy hour entertainment I'd envisioned. I was constantly booting my "neighbors" out for offering services, panhandling, and trying to sell drugs to my customers and employees. One afternoon, one of these tenants, thinking it was his apartment building, passed out in the lobby of *Carol's*. He smelled like a distillery and had a bloody wound on his head. The luncheon crowd stepped over him to enter the restaurant while we waited for the cops. "Whatever you do," I warned them, "don't order the special. Look what happened to him!"

Out in the alley behind the restaurant, we frequently found syringes, human feces, and prostitutes giving johns blow jobs. Drug deals were made out in the open and, on more than one occasion, lowlifes scaled the fire escape on our building, broke windows to the fourth floor, and ransacked the place. There was little there to steal because the room was used mainly for storage. Fortunately, a bolted door kept them from entering the office on the second floor or restaurant on the first.

I also had constant conflict with the next door landlords over keeping their building cleaner. Rats and insects were in abundance from the building's filth and it would be only a matter of time before these pests found their way into *Carol's*. In fact, on one busy Friday night, a partying butch-brother stabbed a rat with a steak knife in the back hall by the bathrooms. The rodent had sneaked in while a dishwasher was taking out the trash.

I tried everything I could think of to deal with the craziness. I visited the mayor several times to see if she could help me with the predicament. She did what she could. She and some city officials put together a raid for the building. For some reason, however, the raid was only to find out the condition of the renters' living space. Why they didn't order a drug raid, I'll never know. While the apartment officials stood outside the building before the "raid" commenced, all the residents ran down the back fire escape with their goods and scurried off like roaches in light. That incursion brought citations for sinks that didn't drain, toilets that hadn't flushed in months, and faulty wiring. Those penalties, however, did nothing to solve my problem.

The police had known for some time that the building was trouble. They'd been called there over and over for domestic violence or to apprehend wanted criminals. The fire department also frequented next door, often because of gas leaks. But the building was a low-income residence where an eviction takes months and even then is nearly unattainable. Even the landlords wanted to get rid of some of the tenants. Unless the cops found absolute proof of any complaint, it boiled down to my word against the person I was protesting. On several occasions, the cops dragged the bad guys away and threw them in jail for a minute or two before letting them go. I had been working downtown for eons and I was aware of transients, panhandlers, and other elements, but this was absurd. One neighbor's photo showed up on *America's Most Wanted*. How's that for prestige?

A Worthless Employee Is Better Than No Employee

The excuses and histrionics from employees not wanting to come to work got bigger, better, and more imaginative when *Carol's* moved up the street. Employing a chef took some pressure off me because it was his job to make sure all bases were covered; however, I still played an active role in making sure they were. We didn't call the Drop Inn Center anymore because their referrals never worked out, but we did call on temporary placement services when we were absolutely desperate.

We nicknamed one little dishwasher Willow. He looked just like a tree-gnome with his long, skinny fingers and his tiny ears that were nearly pointed at the tip. Willow called in sick because he claimed that on his way to work he was instantly blinded. He told us he'd had a hard time feeling his way to a phone booth and had wasted several quarters on dialing wrong numbers. When we told him he must show for work or his position at *Carol's* would disappear as spontaneously as his eyesight, a miracle happened—his vision returned. He began to describe his blurry visions to us over the phone crying out, "I can see! I can see!" I was humbled to have been part of such an awe-inspiring phenomenon.

Ray was another employee. A nice enough guy, meek and quiet, but as slow moving as an arthritic turtle. He was a decent cook, however, and followed directions well. One day, Chef Ken noticed Ray drinking some kind of emerald green liquid. When Ken asked what it was, Ray replied, "Chlorophyll." His explanation was simple enough. Ray said he drank chlorophyll because he believed the Earth was about to be taken over by alien "plant people" and soon we would all be forced to eat chlorophyll. He was simply acclimating his body for the inevitable. From then on we called him Ray-Lian. He mentioned that he would continue to work peacefully at *Carol's* until his starship was ready to leave. All I asked for was a two-week notice—in Earth time.

Then there was an action-packed day when an employee ran into my office, zinging off the walls like a fly trying to get out a window, crying and begging for his entire paycheck in advance. He smacked his hands together like he was praying and actually got down on his knees. I repeatedly told him no. Then he got serious and uncovered the reason he needed his pay so desperately. He explained that when he had walked into his apartment that morning, he'd found his wife in a romantic tryst with another man. He said that he went out of his body and demons took over his soul causing him to stab his wife, her lover, and the dog. He had to leave town right away, he exclaimed. "Why the dog?" I asked. He still had to wait until payday.

Then there were the people I had to hire on the fly to fill space. Most of these "quick hires" turned out for the worse. Finding decent help was a full-time job and the job market was so thin that I had to choose between the lesser of evils. But a worthless employee is at times better than no employee and this guy I'd hired to cook claimed to be able to do so, but...

Each day for lunch we offered specials along with the regular menu. Specials were leftovers that blossomed into simple yet tasty delights. My chef and I urged the day cooks to use leftovers in the specials to cut down on food waste. And what this guy scraped together for a special was indeed waste.

One day I walked into work just as the lunch crowd was beginning to come in full herd. I had already done the usual morning routine of calling a number of times to find out whether deliveries had arrived or what employee was running late or didn't show up at all. On that day though, all were present and accounted for and it seemed an easy start until one of the servers showed me a menu with the mimeographed flyer of the specials tucked inside. She hissed into my ear, "I'm embarrassed to serve this crap! I can't sell this!" *What could be so bad?* I thought to myself before I glanced at the special sheet. Then I read on. The salad du jour was (and this is exactly as the morning lead cook had prepared the flyer)…

Liver Fiesta!
Sliced Baby Liver Sautéed with Green Peppers and Red Onions.
Mixed in a Italian Marinaro Sause
Served over a bed of Wild Rice Pilaf and Mixed Greens
in a Fried Tortilla Shell
Toped with Manchego Cheese
$5.50

She was right. I was embarrassed, too, and couldn't pull the special sheets out of all the menus fast enough. What did he do, scrounge in the dumpster to find the elements for this culinary convulsion? We did serve one of those chef's specials that day…to a lawyer! I made him write and sign a release stating that *Carol's* was not responsible for any interior bodily harm he might suffer through the next millennium. I asked the guy how he could possibly order such hodgepodge and he answered, "It sounded so atrocious that I thought it had to be good." (Shows you what lawyers know!)

A Few Good Turns

This story is dedicated to Elizabeth (Buffy) Munroe-Roberts who gave me another chance and taught me a lesson on forgiving myself.

Having seen a few people straighten out the crooked paths they were on, I began to believe that I could do more than just watch these momentarily employed transients flit in and out of my life. I was certain I could contribute something substantial to people trying to get hold of themselves and their circumstances. Sometimes people just need a second chance—some a tenth one. Sometimes they need someone who believes in them. I knew from personal experience what it was like to be on the receiving end of new chances and to feel the strength of having other peoples' faith in me. If I hadn't, I might not be writing this now. Unfortunately, there were many who didn't want to be listened to.

Marty had been in my employ at the old *Carol's* for about two years. Early one morning, he called me crying. He was in utter despair. His teenage son had been shot and killed in a gang-related shooting in the Cincinnati neighborhood where they lived. I gave Marty $1,000 to pay for his funeral and to buy a burial suit for his son. He and I went to the funeral together and I granted him a week off with pay to get himself together, but he was never the same. He started using crack cocaine. At the time, I wasn't sure whether his unpredictable behavior was caused by alcohol, drugs, depression, or a combination of all three. I repeatedly asked and tried to help him, but he didn't want to be helped. A couple of months after his son was killed, Marty flew off the handle, yelled nonsensically, and quit in the middle of a weekend night.

He came into the restaurant six months after that episode and apologized for his disloyalty and his behavior, admitting he'd been addicted to crack during the time he walked out of *Carol's*. I loved Marty. He had been part of my family and I was happy to see him getting his life back in order. He wasn't asking for his job back. He just wanted me to know he was in a rehab program that made him face the people he had wronged during his addiction. I forgave him. Marty died in 1998, and as far as I know, he died a crack-addicted man.

Johnny was a long-time employee at the little *Carol's* as well. He was smart, responsible, one helluva a line cook, quiet, liked to laugh a lot, and loved belonging to *Carol's* family. My mother brought him presents when she visited. Johnny, too, became addicted to substances. I could feel him moving away from me until one day he didn't show up for work. That wasn't like him at all. I tried getting in touch with him but wasn't successful. A couple of years later, he came into the new *Carol's* to have a heart-to-heart with me. He admitted to an addiction and apologized profusely. He wanted another chance. We gave him that but after two or three weeks, he pulled the same exit scene as he had done a couple of years before.

Another cook, Maurice, was a thirty-something man with face skin as rough as an armadillo shell. He gave me a song-and-dance about how he was down on his luck and was staying in a halfway house because he'd lost everything through a messy divorce. He was particularly neat in appearance with pressed pants, a short-sleeve, oxford-cloth shirt and a tie that was knotted so tight I wondered if it might reflect what was going on inside of him. His brilliantined, straight, dark brown hair was combed to perfection, and his black expressionless eyes seemed almost dead. While he spoke, he habitually rubbed his hands together to keep them from shaking. Even his lips trembled. He had a chance at *Carol's* and was an unbelievably talented cook—more like a chef, blending and creating the best tasting food from the very basic inventory on the shelves of the little *Carol's* basement. But I knew he was another time bomb.

He made gourmet-quality hamburgers that flew out of the kitchen at the speed of light; but one Friday night, they were barely being pattied. I went into the kitchen and smelled his refreshment glass (something I'd gotten used to). It was pure cooking sherry, not even doused with cubes or cola to curb the bad taste. The entire half-gallon of bitter, salty, vinegar wine was drained. I couldn't believe he was still standing. I fired him on the spot.

Two days later, a distinguished, well-dressed, older English gentleman came into *Carol's*. He had learned from the halfway house that his son, the sherry-swiggler, worked for me. When I told him I'd let him go, the ascotted man sank into a chair and cried. Then he took his red silk handkerchief from his tailored suit and told me his story. His son had traveled in England, Japan, and Austria as a concert pianist. He had played at Carnegie Hall and at the Met and at Harvard and Oxford Universities. His talent could still be heard on cassettes. His family tracked him from flop house to flop house, but were unable to reach him.

And then there was "Dan Dan—The Personal Space Invader Man." We called him that because he stood so close to you when talking. It was as if he were trying to climb inside your pores. Dan was a middle-aged man with thinning hair and fractured Coke-bottle glasses that were repaired with tape and bent safety pins. He had a great vocabulary and spoke well and clearly—when he wasn't drinking, that is. What I was told was that Dan and his wife had traveled the world when he was a business executive in a large communications firm.

Now divorced, he lived alone in a decrepit apartment building across the street from my joint, collecting money from the government for God knows what. On his first night at work, he said over and over again how happy he was that he had a job, a place of his own to crash, and that he felt his life was finally coming together. He kept thanking me. Dan asked if he could take a couple of votive candles to use in his apartment because he didn't have electricity and didn't know when he would be able to afford it. This is the stuff that tore my insides out.

Loren was young, tall, nice looking, and was putting himself through college. He was one of the best servers *Carol's* ever employed. He worked multiple double shifts, picked up where others slacked, and never complained. When I saw his happy disposition turn irritable and anxious, the alarm went off inside of me. Then he didn't show for work. That was a first. I called his house and when I finally got hold of him, I asked what was going on his life. He explained that he was stressed with school and had some family problems he was trying to work out. I knew it was more than that, and within a week, Loren was no longer employed at *Carol's*.

He called me some months later and wanted to talk to me. Again, another human being admitted to being addicted to that damn white powder. He said that he was getting himself together and wanted his job back. Working in a party atmosphere is difficult for a person trying to overcome a drug addiction like cocaine. We talked about that at length. I rehired him; but within two weeks, he pulled the same stuff. He was far from throwing the monkey off his back.

It was sad to see people who had so much on the ball and, for whatever reason, lose it and then not be able to piece their lives back together. One young man—smart, handsome, personality-plus, and talented—had worked with me at Rusconi's. The day I hired him, his fellow coworkers referred to him as "The Whip," which made me instantly nervous. On his third day of work at *Carol's*, another employee caught him smoking crack cocaine in the bathroom.

They brought him up to my office and I questioned him about it. His defense was so believable that I nearly doubted the veracity of the employee who busted him. He claimed he was recently married and had a new baby and that he would never put the two people he loved most in the world in such a position. He was a father and a husband and he vowed to God in front of me that he was committed to caring for them the best he could. He even suggested taking a urine test to prove his innocence. I thought that was a good idea and agreed to pay for it.

The results came back. His body was full of cocaine. The next day when I telephoned him to tell him of his failed test, I found his phone disconnected. He showed up some days later to collect his three-day pay. I just prayed that his baby (if he really *had* a baby) would get to eat from his brief earnings. I feared, however, that the money would go up in smoke. What really bothered and frightened me was the total absence of reality to him. Having been somewhat there myself, I can understand how quickly people can get so far away from themselves.

I experienced more of these situations than I care to write about. It's not easy to stay solid and clear in believing when you continually get stampeded and know that you've helped only a few. It is hard on your heart (and sometimes wallet). Though I do know that if someone's road can lead to better beginnings because of just believing in them or by simply listening, then it's worth the world. I read somewhere that it's just possible we are all angels who are put here on Earth to help each other.

Perhaps we are.

SELF-DECAYING

After a couple of years, running the business did get easier. Well, maybe it didn't get easier—maybe I just got used to trauma and upset. But I could feel myself moving farther and farther away from me and all the things I held dear. My colors were fading. I was becoming something I didn't like. I was becoming hard, rough, and worse, unsurprised. The child inside of me was gone. I started to crawl inside myself because everyone wanted a piece of me and there was nothing left over for me.

The taxes required to be in business are like a chronic and worsening disease. There's the payroll tax (which in our case including giving money to two states: Ohio and Kentucky) plus the taxes due the City of Cincinnati and Hamilton County. Then there's FIT/FICA and FUTA and, of course, Workers Compensation, sales tax, personal property tax, estimated tax, inventory tax, unemployment tax, tobacco and firearms tax, quarter-end tax—and that ain't all of 'em.

Then there's boxing with ex-employees who believe they deserve unemployment, personnel records to keep up with, keeping current with the employee handbook, and business insurance. *Carol's* also provided dental and health care for employees who worked twenty-five hours per week, paying half of each monthly premium for hourly staff and full premium for salaried employees. The permits, including the food and liquor licenses, that had to be paid each year were enough to drain a business of all finances alone. Every day, a tax or permit fee was due.

And the codes! How it burned me up knowing what was next door. What a double standard and how unfair those building and health department codes, making sure the broken was always fixed, so an employee wouldn't sue the company for a handrail that had been loose for months. And liabilities! Always praying that employees washed their hands and cooking utensils frequently so as not to contaminate food with bacteria, and praying that all the refrigeration was up to par so food wouldn't spoil. Or the woman who chomped on a Band-Aid that she found in her tuna salad sandwich wouldn't sue me for trauma. Or that an intoxicated customer wouldn't get pulled over or wind up in an accident and blame it on the bartender for serving too many cocktails. Maintenance contracts on top of maintenance contracts to repair cash registers, refrigeration, plumbing, copier, fax machine, and on and on. All of this compounded with the daily crises, including that damn lawsuit.

I felt the rug being pulled from beneath my feet. I had trouble sleeping but when I did sleep, disturbing dreams swarmed mercilessly in my head. I couldn't shut my mind off. My longtime friendship with David Wilson started to strain. With the exception of being in the same office, we didn't see each other and barely spoke. I wasn't having fun anymore. Once open to employees coming to me for whatever reason, I was now closed and quick to yell. They were damned if they came to me and damned if they didn't. I thought about acquiring a *real* business partner to share in the responsibility, but the profit margin was so low I didn't know what I could offer anyone else. Besides, even if things weren't done the right way, it was all done my way. I didn't want to have to answer to anyone else.

ALIEN ASSAULT

I've smoked a lot of pot in my day and swallowed a ton of drugs. At the 1995 anniversary party at *Carol's Corner Café*, we were commemorating five years of business, three at the *Corner* and two at the bigger place. And although I was one hundred percent sober, the evening felt like an acid trip.

It was about seven o'clock in the evening and the place was already jammin' (being busy that early was unusual because the *Carol's* crowd was usually a late night one—unless free hors d'oeuvres and stiff complimentary punch were for the taking). Everyone was there. My Don and a bunch of buddies came down to celebrate and every great customer who had supported me over the years was there...even the ones I didn't like. Then entered Mr. Strawberry.

Mr. Strawberry wasn't his given moniker—he named *himself* after the tasty berry. He was a pleasant man, about sixty years old, who gabbed incessantly about things I could never follow. Mr. Strawberry had red-blonde hair, wore groovy attire, kept his shirt unbuttoned mid-sternum with chest hairs springing through, and a thick gold neck chain with a dangling medallion was like holiday trim on a tree to him. Mr. Strawberry never left his home without his strawberry decals and stickers. He even was author to a pocket-sized book about strawberries, complete with drawings, which he was very proud to show off. One day, Mr. Strawberry came to my office. He was distraught. It turned out that Greg, my assistant manager, kept joking around and calling him Mr. Kiwi and Mr. Kumquat and Mr. Banana. Mr. Strawberry didn't find the fruit calling the least bit humorous. The only fruit he desired to be called was Mr. Strawberry and he wanted that other *nonsense* to stop immediately. What could I do but inform Greg to only refer to the gentleman as Mr. Strawberry?

This particular night, Mr. Strawberry made his entrance to the anniversary party wearing a full-body, bright red, foam rubber strawberry with seeds painted on it. He embellished this attire with white gloves, green tights, and a brown beret with a large stem sprouting from the middle. And he carried his heavily strawberry-decaled boom box. I told him how festive he looked and he claimed that he had worn this outfit *just* for me in order to properly celebrate *Carol's* fifth year of business.

I guess I felt honored—but I didn't get it.

Was this get-up like his tuxedo or something? As I searched my brain for any possible connection between strawberries and *Carol's Corner Café*, he asked me to turn down the jukebox (he always said the "boom-boom" music was too loud). I thought he was going to make a speech because his hands shook a bit. But as the bartender lulled the music, Mr. Strawberry set his boom box on a high-top table. With his white gloved hands, like a magician pulling a rabbit out of a hat, he presto-pushed the "on" button which was cued to a cassette of Carol Channing blaring "Hello Dolly."

I still didn't get it.

Then he snatched up my hand, waved it high in the air as though I were the champion prize fighter, and marched me around my restaurant, interjecting "Hello *Carol*" to each "Hello Dolly." He just lip-synched the rest of the words. When the song ended, he stood, spongy, seedy, and red, and quite pleased with himself as onlookers smiled, but we were all confused and nobody knew whether they should clap or not. He then put a white baseball cap with a sequined jalapeno pepper appliqué stitched on the front of it on my head. I hugged the genetically altered berry and thanked him for whatever had just happened to me.

And I *still* didn't get it.

About two hours after Mr. Strawberry's pageant, a woman I'd known for years rolled on the scene. She was in a wheelchair as a result of a car accident, even though she could walk (I knew this) but, being somewhat loony and an intense drama queen, she would go to great lengths to get attention. When she wheeled in that night, she was hostile. I knew it wasn't going to be pretty.

Like a ricocheting pinball, she deliberately rammed into the backs of people's legs, plowed into tables, knocked over chairs and stools, and made quite a fracas. Pandemonium on casters! A few customers griped about her behavior but then apologized for complaining about a woman in a wheelchair. I knew I had to do something. I was sitting with Larry Eynon and Don Beck and asked for their opinions over this absurd dilemma when she locomotived up from behind and crashed into their table so hard that their wine glasses toppled over. "Oops!" she said sarcastically, "I'm sorry! It's just that these aisles are *so* narrow!" Then she went and parked herself at a table. That's when I knew, wheelchair or not, the broad had to go.

I collected myself to make sure I'd not show any nastiness, walked over to her table, bent down to her ear, and whispered very politely that she must leave. Like a freshly punctured oil well, she spewed up from the chair, slapped my face and then started karate kicking me in the stomach. Patrons were wholly bewildered and didn't know how to react. It was as if the Incredible Hulk had just shredded through his clothes and stood green and brawny and growling directly in front of them. The look of astonishment was on all their faces and I could read their thoughts: *Should I help Carol and engage in combat with a woman in a wheelchair? How would that look? What will people think?* She delivered another swift Bruce Lee kick and I fell back into a customer's lap. I must have looked like one of those plastic punching clowns that pop back up after you hit 'em, because the lap owner's reflex pushed me back into her perimeter of sparring limbs. I just stood there, dodging her strikes, dazed. I remember thinking, *a...woman...in ... a ... wheelchair ... is ... beating ... me ... up.*

I didn't hit back. I'm not a fighter (midgets aside, of course). I'm sure it would have looked aces rolling on the floor in my brand new, $200 floral dress and heels fighting some broad in a wheelchair. Like the rest of my guests, I just couldn't see it. I screamed for Greg to get her off me and he, Larry, and other *Carol's* associates pried her away from me and held her at bay. By this time, Don heard the hoopla and hurried to defend his bride. They forced her back onto her wheelchair and when they tried to carry her and it outside, she blocked the door frame with her arms and very strong and very able legs. She looked like a tarantula clinging to the edges of a vacuum hose before getting sucked in. A group of partygoers were clapping and chanting over and over, "Praise Jesus! Thank the

Lord! It's a miracle! She is cured! Praise Jesus! Thank the
Lord! It's a Miracle! She is cured! Praise Jesus..."

She cycled back and forth on the sidewalk by *Carol's* front
windows flipping us the bird while Larry, David Wilson, Greg,
and my Don stayed outside with her so she wouldn't reenter
the arena. We called for the police to take her away, but she'd
already made tracks up the street by the time they arrived. As
we talked to the officers, they received a call requesting their
assistance for a disturbance at a bar a couple of blocks away. It
seemed that it involved a woman in a wheelchair and that
when some other cops were trying to put her in the paddy
wagon, she went berserk again and started to pound on them,
forcing them to restrain with handcuffs a mentally deranged,
physically-non-handicapped woman in a wheelchair. Earlier,
I'd been concerned that it was just me. But then I knew not to
take her attack personally.

COME TO THE CABARET

*For Tommy Lawson, Larry Eynon, Don Beck , Jim McCormick, and
David Adams for helping make my dream a reality.*

So with all the rubbish I had crammed in my head that made
me manic and completely unsynchronized, what do you think I
did? After two crazed years in the new spot, I built my dream
of the second floor cabaret room. With lunacy surging from
every pore of my body, I thought that if I could do something I
really wanted to do (like entertain), it would add some balance
and levity to my chaotic life. Plus, by singing in my own
honky-tonk, nobody could fire me! More loans. Further
in debt.

Although I was convinced the upstairs was supposed to happen, my dream was a horrible business decision. While the restaurant was usually busy, I had trouble making a dime. I was a lame businessperson, usually shooting from my hip, making radical decisions without consulting my management, not planning things out well enough. The business was already in a financial stretch when I piggybacked more debt for the loan to build the second floor.

The construction was already underway and the loan for building the cabaret was nearly clinched. Then the financial institution read the fine print and learned of the ongoing lawsuit. Many times, my attorney thought it would disappear, but the damned thing would lie dormant for months, then contaminate my busy life every time Fred felt like rocking my world. Banks don't like lending dough to small corporations with an active lawsuit and there was the terrifying prospect that they might back out. Thank God the loan officer believed in me—just further proof that no one can sell me like I can sell myself (well, the fact that the loan officer was a golfing buddy of Don's didn't hurt). Eventually, the loan was approved.

This wasn't going to be a mere cabaret room, it would be the *premiere* cabaret room. I had visualized throughout the years that my music room would eventually come to be. I'd even gone to auctions and collected chandeliers, round lounge booths, brass railings—anything that looked like it would fit in my dream. Don Beck designed the space, adding red, velvet drapes with big, gold-rope tassels and a black-and-white ceramic tile floor that circled the bar. He and Larry bought three huge, antique mirrors and we painted the wood-carved frames gold. Don suggested a floor-to-ceiling mirror on the wall behind where the band would be stationed, but I couldn't afford the added expense. So they bought it as a grand opening present. They, too, had a vision of this room. It was going to be finer than the Algonquin Room in Manhattan! The centerpiece would be my mother's Steinway baby grand piano that she got for her eighth birthday (I had it shipped from Tucson). I commissioned a local artist to paint a mural of piano keys dancing around the room. Stepping into this vision would be like walking into *Rick's Café Americain* in Casablanca. With practically no effort at all, you would be able to see Humphrey Bogart with his cigarette, wearing his white jacket and black bow tie, leaning against the bar and sipping a highball.

When the carpet was being installed about a week prior to opening, my attorney's associate came by with some papers for me to sign. As he walked out of my office, he slipped on some wet glue the carpet layer had just spread out. But he didn't just slip—he rolled in the sticky stuff, ruining his black leather briefcase and his shirt and tie and new slacks and jacket that he'd just had tailored. Although I must declare it was somewhat gratifying to see a lawyer quiver about like a mosquito stuck in the hot wax of a citronella candle, the fulfillment dispersed as I wrote him a check for his epoxy-damaged clothes. I gather I could not have reimbursed him and told him to jump on the lawsuit brigade—but I really didn't want to be sued by my own attorney.

The great thing about the construction was that I hired a knowledgeable foreman and things were done correctly. That felt awesome. I hired the electrical contractors, the painters, and the plumbers. I learned how to read bids and contracts. I made all the decisions. I was also blessed with a marvelous group of volunteer help including Bill, Sue, and Sandy. They refinished my mother's piano and the back bar and built the front bar, and Paula inlayed a gorgeous mosaic floor with her handmade tiles. Don Beck and Larry Eynon did a multitude of things, including painting the back hallway till three o'clock in the morning right before the opening. Everyone wanted this place to live. Family was continuing and that re-lit a candle inside of me. I still did a lot of the physical labor but for me, it was truly a labor of love. I was going to be a chanteuse in my own fabu room!!!

LIFE IS NOT ALWAYS A CABARET

For Curtis Overcash, Jean Toepfert and David Hughes, who helped keep the dream alive. And Tammy White and Jen Nesbitt who were the glue that held the downstairs together.

Rob and Steve formulated an astrological chart for the birthday of *Upstairs at Carol's* and we scheduled the opening for August 9, 1996. This baby was born a Leo with Gemini rising to make it fun, versatile, ever-changing, and dramatic, which is exactly what it would be. And Tommy Lawson was the man qualified to make it happen.

I had hired Tommy to bartend downstairs, with the intention of moving him upstairs as the stage director when we opened. This was his dream, too. He had more than thirteen years of professional experience with stage productions and was well-connected with the theatrical community. Tommy and I put together our band and we called ourselves "Carol and the Socialites."

Five months before the upstairs opened, we had the pianist, drummer, bass player, and me. I wasn't experienced enough (nor did I want to) to carry two forty-five-minute shows by myself on weekend nights as Tommy had planned. I needed a strong singing partner, someone who could do duets with me and sing solos, and someone who was confident and knew enough about the trade to teach me the ins and outs. Besides singing in the choruses as a teenager in community theatre and singing in the Ron Stephens Benefits and being asked to belt out a song or two at charity functions, I didn't have much seasoning in performing. But I knew I wanted to. I wanted to sing. And I wanted a partner.

Our first tryout seemed dandy, but he soon showed his monster-side. This guy was in it all for himself, along with his nasty temper. Nobody wanted to work with him. He screamed, threw diva fits, and tried to intimidate everyone in the band. Two months prior to opening the second floor, we goat-butted him from the group. The next day, he repeatedly called my answering machine at home, shouting obscenities, calling me a "dumb kike" and "cheap Jew" and laughing insanely like a mad scientist from some low-budget 1930s horror movie. He claimed Hitler was correct in using the skin of Jews for lamp-shades. My Don wanted to meet with him to knock his block off, but thank goodness the sensible-maniac rejected Don's overtures. One evening, out on his own partying at a bar, our own five-foot six-inch Chef Ken was antagonized by the six-foot-plus, gay, anti-Semitic, cabaret singer and punched his lights out. A cop friend of mine helped me get a restraining order, but this guy turned out to be just full of hot air. Within days, he'd deflated and disappeared.

Our next audition was a Hawaiian-cowboy country singer who accompanied himself on ukulele. And that's all folks. No one else applied. Finally, as we really started to panic, a young woman came along who wanted to join the band. I'd known

her for several years from her participation in *Carol's* benefits
but because of my own lack of confidence, I didn't want a
girl to perform alongside of me. I didn't want to be compared
to her.

This woman called me at home and begged me to give her
a chance. She told me she understood my concerns and I was-
n't being fair to myself if I didn't give her a go. She pointed out
that we had totally different vocal styles which would only add
to the show. She said that it was crazy for me to be insecure. I
knew she was right. She was just what we were looking for
and I was standing in the way of it happening. Tommy leveled
with me, too. How could I continue hiding from myself?

She was in, and Tommy and I thought we had finally figured out the perfect formula. The band was solid, my infring-
ing insecurities vanished, and it felt like people couldn't wait to
get upstairs to spend their cash. It was the buzz.

Under the artistic and watchful eye of the band's stage
director, choreographer, spotlight dude, lighting technician,
chandelier duster and bulb-changer, prop master, costume
designer, promotional director, carpet cleaner, friend (AKA
Tommy), "Carol and the Socialites" performed two shows
every Friday and Saturday night at *Upstairs at Carol's* for six
months. We sang Broadway tunes and standards and filled in
the gaps with a touch of camp, vaudeville, and burlesque. We
got rave reviews from the media and the audiences, but we
weren't getting enough paying patrons in the door.

The first thing we did was slice the upstairs overhead.
Then it became difficult keeping employees upstairs because of
the lack of tips. The ones who did choose to remain did so for
the simple love of the place, and their determination helped
keep me pluggin' on. Shortly after, we ixnayed the appetizer

menu because the food wasn't going over that grand. Down
the line, we saved even more money by doing the janitorial
work ourselves.

In spite of the money deficit, *Upstairs at Carol's* was a nucle-
us for fine entertainment. Some big names performed upstairs
when they were in town. After their paid performances, they
would sometimes give impromptu late-evening appearances
and would collect money for charities like Broadway Cares/
Equity Fights AIDS. Betty Buckely appeared in my room
after a performance, and composer/singer/Broadway starlet
Ann Hampton Callaway performed in my beautiful dream
room not once, but twice. A highlight of my life will always be
when we sang *As Time Goes By* together at the piano for Larry
Eynon's fiftieth birthday party.

The touring cast of *Sunset Boulevard* put on two delightful
cabaret shows and raised a lot of money for Broadway Cares.
We also held a political campaign cabaret featuring tons of
local celebrities (including myself!) to re-elect the mayor of
Cincinnati. I lent the space many times to the Cincinnati Men's
Chorus for their fund-raising concerts.

Meanwhile, my absence downstairs was tough on the
restaurant. Customers missed me and even some employees
yearned for my mug. And it was hard for my managers, David
and Greg, who worked more hours for no added pay. I must
admit I missed running the restaurant. I loved kibitzing with
customers and friends.

GEMINIS CAN BE IN TWO PLACES AT THE SAME TIME...CAN'T WE?

I had to figure out a way to both sing upstairs and manage downstairs. When I was upstairs performing, I was concerned about what was happening in the restaurant. When I was in the restaurant, I was thinking about upstairs. I couldn't give a hundred percent to either place. When audiences were light, I counted the number of heads and my stomach churned wondering how I was going to pay the entertainment *and* the employees *and* the ASCAP and BMI royalties and the admission tax for the cover charge. Although I had capable managers taking care of the café, I felt it needed me. After all, it was me.

Tommy auditioned other bands to play upstairs on the weekends and rotated cabaret shows so I'd be able to work in the restaurant when we weren't performing. That also enabled Tommy to work downstairs on those nights to make some money bartending. In the initial plans, he was supposed to get a percentage of the door profits but it never happened, because we didn't have any.

Then trouble with the band started. Instead of being the team we were months before, we started pulling away from one another. Some band members thought I had ulterior motives, that I was being secretive. They began to resent me. That left Tommy twisted in all directions. Even rehearsals were tough. I was plagued with phone calls and often summoned downstairs to help. I started to resent *Carol's Corner Café* and the upstairs as well. The two entities had pirated my life.

We dropped the cover charge to many shows just to get people in the door. Often I had to snag money from the registers downstairs to pay the bands and that put a tighter vice on finances. David Wilson came up with another way to generate some cash flow upstairs. Since the place was so cool-looking and felt comfortable to sit in, he thought customers would love to sip on cocktails upstairs while listening to hip music spun from CDs. He picked Thursday nights to start out with and if it was popular, we could always add more nights. One bartender and one server were all that was needed, so overhead would be low. David thought a tarot card reader wandering about would be an excellent touch.

It was a great vision, but basically all it did was steal customers from the bar downstairs (and on Tommy's bartending night no less!). The card reader proved to be quite popular and made more money than we did. On a Thursday night in January 1997, I asked her to read my cards. She said that I'd be at *Carol's* for six months to a year because there were other things for me to do. I thought she was a mixed-up medium and almost demanded my money back. How is it possible that I'd be there for such a short time? I had just taken on the national debt to build upstairs! I even had begged my landlord to rewrite the ten-year lease making it for fifteen years because that would allow me more time to build profits from the additional capital *Carol's* put into his building. Six months to a year? She had also mentioned that she saw a legal matter in my cards and that it would continue for some time, but it would be over when I handed a lump sum of money over to a large man.

We decided to close Thursday night gatherings upstairs in March. It was silly to remain open since there wasn't any business. I honestly thought the addition of the Cabaret Room would make money for *Carol's* and that my being able to entertain would improve my lousy disposition. Just the opposite was happening. Building the upstairs turned out to be as disastrous as having a baby to save a marriage. Heavy anxiety and heart palpitations besieged me for days on end. Something was happening to me internally. No joke, I thought I was ready to be hospitalized. Between rehearsals, performing, selling the upstairs for private parties, finagling sparse finances, the lawsuit, managing the restaurant downstairs, scheduling employees to work two floors, dealing with members of the band, finding alternative acts for upstairs, and the daily turbulence that comes with the territory, I was turning inside out.

I was also hurt by the number of people I knew who were dying of AIDS. Every day, I was faced with another person who was newly diagnosed or who was on his way out of this world. I could no longer handle the masses of people who were sick. I got to the point that I just couldn't stand to hear about it anymore. All those benefits we held to assist in AIDS organizations seemed worthless. There seemed no end in sight. Worse, my accountant told me that *Carol's* could no longer afford to continue giving the $50 donation with every death. Everything was caving in on me. I was unraveling. And when the head honcho unscrews, everything else falls in the same fashion.

Maybe it *is* time for me to move on…

In addition to the names I've already mentioned, our Earth also lost in a short time in my small corner of the world:

Don Blaine, Phil Bollinger, Billy Bolyard, Michael Dorobeck,
David Fischer, Jeff Gundrum, Robert Halenbeek, Sam Hall,
John Harden, Tom Hart, Gregory Landrum, Gary Martin,
Michael McDaniel, Steve Patton, Randy Root, Alan Saunders,
Clarence Smith, Ed Stephenson, Glenn Thomas,
Robbie Wetzel, Michael Zachary...

Encore!

BEEN THERE, DONE THAT...
NOW GET ME THE HELL OUT!

I had a mental breakdown in May 1997. Everything fell apart all at once. I couldn't sleep more than two or three hours a night and my slight eating disorder, which had been under control for the most part, came back into full bloom. (I'm a binge eater. I used to purge every once in a while in my late teens and early twenties, but purging was never truly my gig.) I was physically shaking, and I had itchy blotches of rash all over my body and acne on my face, I felt anxious and irrational, my moods were wild and hysterical crying fits hit me in force. I was having two periods a month. I bit my nails down to the quick and my fingers were sore and bleeding. I lost all interest in sex. My skin didn't feel like mine and it sometimes felt like all of my nerve endings were exploding rockets. I had difficulty talking in full sentences and my mind couldn't focus on a single thought.

For the first time in the history of *Carol's*, I missed a week of work. I was afraid to leave my house. I didn't even feel competent enough to drive my car. During that work week missed, I stayed around the house and gardened and cried to my parents on the phone all day and when Don came home from work, I cried to him. I didn't know what was wrong with me. I thought in my heart that I was over the edge. I was frightened that I'd never return.

My concerned and frustrated husband urged me (to put it nicely) to see a doctor. For the past several months, Don had been living in hell with me. (Note to the Universe: Thank you for dropping into my arms such a supportive, loving man.) The one thing I knew that was solid and real was his continued and devoted love for me. I didn't think a doctor could help, but even I knew I needed something, so I went. My physician observed not only how my behavior was at that moment, but wanted a full history of it. One thing that was never a problem was talking about myself!

Ever since I was very young, I've always either soared high in the sky or wallowed in quicksand-filled black holes. I've never been able to find a happy medium, a place where it's okay to be sad and yet not pull yourself further down or to be content with the good times and not hyper out. This episode was different. It wasn't going away. I couldn't bring myself out of it. Bring myself out of it? Hell, I couldn't even *find* myself.

Dr. Gina Grove diagnosed clinical depression and made it clear that I had always been like this. This behavior, she explained, had not just popped out of nowhere and, when extreme stress entered my life, it hit me tenfold. It was time I got hold of it instead of it holding me.

Through the use of prescribed antidepressants and non-addictive sleeping aids, I began feeling *me* again. At first, I hated and was frightened by the thought of using drugs to control my behavior. As my doc put it, "If you were diabetic, you would be taking insulin, wouldn't you?" My brain lacked serotonin, the chemical that allows us to feel good and relax. She explained it was a physical problem and that made it even more acceptable. I started out on Prozac and Ambion, and they worked for a while. Two months later, however, I crashed again. This time, we tried Serzone and Amitriptyline, and they clicked. Then she suggested that I speak with a therapist. Now I thought *she* was nuts!

Therapy is not for everyone just like every alcoholic doesn't need Alcoholics Anonymous in order to quit drinking. The medication was working for me and for the first time in my life, I was able to find an equilibrium—my concentration was coming back, the rash and itchiness cleared, and my eating disorder was under control. I actually started smiling again! I was sleeping better, but was still haunted by nightmares of tornadoes, fires, sinking ships, and of driving cars that were swerving off the road or not going where I was steering. I knew in my heart of hearts that drugs were not the only answer for my problems. Something inside of me needed unearthing to be healed. Perhaps issues with my father? Being angry with myself for all the pain I caused others? The pain I'd caused myself through my past lifestyle?

"Carol and the Socialites" performed the last cabaret show in July 1997 and we closed *Upstairs at Carol's* altogether at the end of the month. Tommy resumed his former position as a full-time bartender downstairs. It was pure heartache for both of us yet at the same time, it was a relief in many ways.

In August, even before I made the call to Dr. Kathryn Ferner (the therapist Doc Grove had recommended), I knew I didn't want to be a restaurant owner anymore. It was time to let her go. What was the point of my staying in a workplace where I was miserable and thus made everyone around me miserable as well? I felt as though my work at *Carol's* had been completed. The Universe was telling me to leave, that there was different work for me to do. In retrospect, I can see that the Universe had been telling me that for a long time; I just wasn't listening.

The tarot card reader who had read my cards back in January was dead on. I wasn't going to be the owner of *Carol's Corner Café* much longer. I just hoped she was wrong about the lump sum of money I was supposed to give to a large man!

EAT TWO, THEY'RE SMALL

I have an eating disorder. So owning a restaurant is a lot like an alcoholic owning a cocktail lounge. One of the reasons I was so stubborn about acquiring a more expansive menu with the bigger *Carol's* was because I was scared. I had grown accustomed to the old stuff on the menu and feared that additional food would just tempt me even more. Was that rational? Probably not, but that's how the addiction manipulated my mind.

There's a black-and-white photograph that hangs in my bathroom. I'm quite partial to it. It shows the bare back of a woman who appears to be in her thirties. Her light hair is tucked into a loose bun on the top of her head with strands of hair falling down the nape of her neck. Her curvaceous body, down to beneath the small of her back, is shadowed by her own flesh. This woman has pronounced rumples of ivory skin on the sloping sides of her body. She is not petite. She does not possess the body of a Victoria's Secret model. And yet she is sexier than a Rubenesque goddess.

When I first saw this photograph in 1991, I fell in love with it. I felt that I was "one" with this heavenly, full-bodied woman. She was stunning and suddenly I realized that I must be stunning, too.

Food has always been my friend. It's always been cordial, never yelling at me, never talking back. It never failed to show up for a date. It never rejected or belittled me. Best of all, it was instantly accessible and reliable and never demanded that I answer to it. Some people eat only when they're hungry. Not me. When I was simply sad or lonely or premenstrual or perhaps when I'd had a great day at *Carol's* or a perfectly horrid one, for that matter—any reason would do—food fulfilled and satisfied me, at least for a moment. Then I craved more.

During my preteen years while the rest of the household slept, I'd devour anything I could get my hands on: a *loaf* of bread, a *can* of black olives, a *box* of cereal. I remember as a young girl going over to friends' homes for supper. Everyone would usually be given nice little portions of whatever made up the meal—a *small* amount of meat, a *little* helping of starch, a *few* vegetables. The most amazing thing was that sometimes people would leave stuff on their plates when they were finished eating. I couldn't understand why. They said it was because they were full. What does "full" mean? What does "full" feel like?

I didn't know I had a problem. I do remember being afraid of not getting enough food. When I went out to restaurants, it didn't matter what I really wanted to eat. I always looked for the entrées with the biggest portion and the most side dishes. Later, I realized that there would never be "enough" and that my voracious eating habit never had anything to do with being hungry.

Since I was never actually obese, I didn't think this eating "thing" of mine warranted talking with anyone about it. Well, that and the fact I was embarrassed that I couldn't control my own eating. I mean, how stupid is that? Millions of people have real problems like drug and alcohol addiction and AIDS and homelessness. Untold numbers of people are abused every day of the year. And my problem is that I can't say no to a Twinkie? It sounded absolutely ridiculous. How could I ask for help with something so trivial?

What I learned from Dr. Ferner though was that if it affects your life negatively, it's a problem. In the past, I've canceled outings with friends and family because of my "need" to stay home and binge, and I've called in sick because my stomach was so messed up from consuming way too much food. I've cried trillions of angry, lonely tears.

I hated myself for it.

Having an eating disorder is hard to deal with because since you have to eat to live, you're confronted by food every day. I had to find control. When I finally realized that what I thought to be a small glitch in my life was indeed a real problem, I went through a grieving process. No matter how I felt after bingeing, I always looked forward to the ritual. I'd get hyped and my body would actually tingle with excitement. It was a familiar, sacred place for me that I shared with no one. When I faced my problem and began to take it day by day trying not to binge, I no longer had the charge that filled my head all day. The anticipation and excitement were gone. It was sad and it was scary. I was lonesome. It's very much like how a heavy smoker feels when he quits smoking.

With the help of the medication to keep me "even" and the assistance of my beloved Dr. Ferner, I discovered that I had been punishing myself for things I'd done in the past and neglecting my spirituality. I had issues with my father that I never resolved and the frustrations and the neglected feelings I had from him manifested into an eating disorder when I was young because I didn't know how to verbalize my emotions. I had to heal. I had to learn to forgive myself for the past. I had to forgive and accept my father. I realized that I had been crying out for people to accept me for a long, long time, but I hadn't been accepting myself. Now I do. I am *me*, the whole ball of wax. I accept in me the good and the not so good.

In my past, I schlepped around trying every diet. The Atkins Diet, Weight Watchers, Jenny Craig, eating only red-colored foods, eating all I wanted before three o'clock in the afternoon and nothing after, drinking gallons of water with meals to fill me up, amphetamines to curb my appetite, protein shakes—you name it, I tried it…for at least a week or so. Then when the plan didn't work, I'd punish myself all over again.

Now that I have some control, I've found the only thing that works for me is to modify a plan that *I* can follow. Everybody is different. Everybody has a different metabolism. Everybody has a different schedule. Everybody is built differently. Everybody has different eating habits. Everyone has to find a personal plan.

I ain't poifect. I have my days (sometimes my weeks), but I have reconciled that this is something I'll *always* have to deal with. It's also something I *can* control. And even though I have owned up to having a problem and dealt with this demon face-to-face, I still wake up with it every morning and go to bed with it every night. But I've learned I can have my cake and eat it, too.

Now I'm a size twelve, sometimes a fourteen, and for a moment I was a ten. But as I look back, people have loved me no matter what my size. Their choice to like or dislike me had nothing to do with added poundage. I met Don when I was a size sixteen. And wouldn't you know it? No matter what my size, he continues to love me. I've felt sexy when I was a size ten and sexy at a size sixteen. It all has to do with how you feel about yourself.

Don't get me wrong. If you and I happen to share some similar woes past or present, I'm not saying you should follow my agenda. You must find your own yellow brick road. Pick and choose. Just remember, it's your mind and soul that are craving to be fulfilled…not your stomach.

MERCURY BABY, SWING MY WAY!

Mercury is the planet in charge of communications and Mercury retrograde (spinning backwards) is the Universe's way of slowing us down and telling us to watch what and how things are communicated. Mercury goes retrograde about three times a year and lasts almost three weeks each time. Astrologers say it's not good to sign important documents or move forward with major decisions during these periods. Instead, it's a time to clean up old stuff.

When I told Paula of my intent to sell the restaurant, she was thrilled for me. Rob and Steve believed it was my time to move on to embrace other dreams. My manager David Wilson and assistant manager Greg both wanted out as badly as I did, but they had done the same thing for so long, they were comfortable with being miserable since that way, at least they knew what to expect. Although Greg is definitely a man who would "go down with his ship," he was ready for a lifeboat. David was going through his own personal hell at that time plus our friendship was in tatters, so communication was not our strongest thread. Although I think he hated *Carol's* as much as I did, it was very difficult for him to welcome change. Mom, Dad, and my sister Nancy couldn't have been happier with my decision. They had seen me evaporate and couldn't wait for me to reappear.

When I told Don, he was a little nervous. He told me that maybe I just needed a break or maybe I should think about acquiring *real* partners to get some weight off my back. As he always said, "If it were easy, everybody would be doing it." I heard what he said but wanted no part of his offered alternatives. I wanted out and I wanted out completely. He soon understood. I think he was apprehensive because all he'd ever known me as was a restaurant owner.

He was also concerned, and rightfully so, that he would have to make up for the attention I was so used to getting at the café. "You're not gonna like, wait for me to come home every day to play *are you?*" I told him not to worry, that there was so much I wanted to do with my time. I wanted a life. I wanted to be home on weekend nights. I wanted to audition for plays. I wanted to build a greenhouse. I wanted to see my stepdaughter and my friends. I wanted to sing in nightclubs. I wanted to take a writing class or radio broadcasting at a college or both. I didn't plan to sit around the house after I sold the place and wear pink, fuzzy slippers while eating bonbons and watching the soaps on TV.

Of course, I had genuine concerns about selling the place. Still, it felt so right in my gut that I knew it was supposed to be. When I finally listened to my intuition to sell, my life just started to clear up and things happened easily and naturally. My dreams were pleasant and positive and full of opportunities. Selling was the only thing that made sense to me. Besides, my fried-to-a-crisp attitude might have put *Carol's* under if I'd continued.

But what would happen to all the employees? Would they be guaranteed jobs by a new owner? I worried about what would happen when word leaked out. Would the employees run in search of other jobs and the clientele base drop? What would happen to David and Greg who had been loyal to *Carol's* since her incarnation? And Chef Ken and dear Tommy who had been anchors and fantastic fellow dreamers in making *Carol's Corner* and the Cabaret Room fly. Was I just going to tell them they no longer had a job? How could I just dispose of all the sound employees so easily? And what about the clientele? *Carol's* was "home" for so many people and I remembered how torn people were when Rusconi's closed. Would the owner-to-be even want to keep the same crowd? Would they be booted and forced to go elsewhere? But where else could they go? *Carol's* was one of a kind! And who would buy this place? I was so embittered towards the restaurant business, I couldn't imagine anyone would actually want to get into it. All of these were valid questions, but I still had to get out. This place was slowly but absolutely strangulating my life. There was no other solution.

I considered hiring a restaurant broker and even spoke to one about assisting me with the sale, but it burned me up to give a broker ten percent of the asking price. I decided to manage the sale of my café by myself. I owed hundreds of thousands of dollars to banks and food suppliers and was delinquent on many of my bills. *Carol's* monthly bank statements regularly had hundreds of dollars added for bounced check fees. My accountant helped me get a financial prospectus together and came up with an asking price and my attorney typed up agreement papers for prospective buyers. Two parties who seemed interested didn't come through.

Although most of my management team was aware of my plans, others only sensed something was up. We pretty much kept selling *Carol's* a secret. One evening, Chef Ken came over to me all smiley and said, "Why don't you ask Marc if he wants it?"

I'd not thought of that. Marc was my daytime supervisor, ran the floor, and did a lot of the banking for the company. He was familiar with the weekly, monthly, and quarterly taxes, payroll, and all the other financial and legal cargo that *Carol's* carried. He knew how hard I worked so he wasn't blind to the demands of the business. He'd started at *Carol's* four years earlier as a busboy, was made a bartender, and then promoted to daytime supervisor. He was a go-getter, a smart and ambitious twenty-five-year-old kid with an inheritance. Why not?

The night in September 1997 when Ken put the bug in my ear, I told Marc about putting the restaurant up for grabs and I asked whether he was interested. His thick, black eyebrows almost raised off his face and a spark charged his dark eyes. He said he and his father had been discussing going into business together *and* his father just happened to be in town for a few days and was waiting downstairs for Marc to join him for dinner. Marc barreled down to tell him about this business proposition. There are no coincidences.

Marc and his dad were quite high on the idea of purchasing *Carol's*. His dad asked if they could have a month or so to think about it and also if I would refrain from showing the café to other interested parties in the meantime. I agreed and they signed a letter of intent to purchase. If they bought the place, they would bring in their own managers, but they would keep the same hourly employees, cater to the same clientele, and would keep "Carol" as part of the name. Everything was moving along smoothly.

While in Arizona for Thanksgiving with my family, I received a call from Marc. He announced that he and his dad were going for the gusto! The two of them plus a third partner would be the new owners of *Carol's*. The whole deal just seemed to fit. It was smooth as silk from the beginning—nothing was hidden, there was no squabbling for the asking price. I had a lot to be thankful for that Thanksgiving.

We set the closing date for February 16, 1998. After conferring with Rob and Steve, however, we postponed it two days. Although those two days felt like two months, I was told not to sign legal documents before Mercury got out of retrograde. It would do so on the morning of February 18. Since they bought the name, the contract had a clause stating that I could not open another *Carol's Corner* within five years or within a five-mile radius of the existing *Carol's*. I had no problem with that. Marc and his dad asked me to make myself available to assist with this transition and I obliged. My future was in launching mode.

We then made the restaurant staff and customers aware that Marc was going to be the successor and everyone was pleased that she would stay in the family. Ken would remain chef at *Carol's*, Greg was offered another job, and David had decided he was going to move out of town in the next few months. I sold the restaurant in its entirety, with the exception of my mother's Steinway, my Betty Boop memorabilia, some sound equipment from upstairs, the spotlight (of course!), and a few other possessions. I'll never forget standing on a barstool and taking down my Boop relics from the shelf that Sue and Bill made for me. As I packed them away in boxes, I was meditative—remembering where I was in business at the time when someone gave me this Boop or that Boop. As I did, a few tears ran down my cheeks.

CONNECTED AND READY TO RECEIVE

Dr. Ferner helped me shear away a few layers of lifeless wool that had been weighing me down. She helped me profoundly in three areas: confronting and accepting my eating disorder, confronting and accepting my father, and letting go of the anger and guilt I had towards myself from the past. That last one was the tough one. I had to end those growth-oppressing emotions and forgive myself instead of berating myself. Whatever occurred in the past is still (and always will be) part of me, it's what made me me. And I like me! I'm still far from having a clean slate (if that's ever possible). I know I'll always have something to contend with; but if I don't, I'll have to be careful not to be freaked out wondering why I don't!

During the last few days of my run at *Carol's*, Amy Culbertson, a columnist with *The Cincinnati Post* called to ask me some questions. She'd heard I was selling the joint and wanted to do a little story on the changeover. One of her questions was, "With the restaurant out of your life, what are you going to do?"

At the time, I hadn't a clue what my future focus would be. The only thing I could think about was leaving with Don for a Hawaiian vacation that had been planned long before I put *Carol's* up for sale (perfect timing, again). I wasn't concerned with what I would be doing for a living in the near future. I knew it would come to me. I knew that if I waited and listened intently with my inner ear, I would be directed. Because she didn't get an immediate response, she repeated her question.

"So Carol...what are you going to do now?"

I blurted out that I was going to write a book. I turned around to see who said that...and much to my surprise, it was me! Hmmm, write a book? I'd always loved writing short stories, but I hadn't thought about writing a book.

"You're writing a book?" she inquired. "Great! What's the title?"

Title? Crap! How the hell did I know what the title would be? I didn't even know I was going to be writing a book until about thirty seconds ago! Without missing a beat and as if this had been on my agenda forever, I said confidently, "*My Life as a Gay Man in a Straight Woman's Body.*"

She thought that was one of the funniest things she'd ever heard while I just sat there wondering where it had come from. I immediately recognized that this was what my inner ear had been training for. I smiled and thought to myself, *Man, I've barely jumped off the work-trolley and my brain is already spiraling up the tracks to begin another project.* Her story was in the paper the following week.

When I came home from hula skirt shopping a few days before vacation and also after my luxurious retirement, I received a phone call from a woman I had never met. She introduced herself and said she was familiar with me and had been a patron in my restaurant. She said she'd read the article in the newspaper and was interested in publishing my book.

A book I hadn't written...yet.

Look, Ma...Two Keys!

It was beyond ecstasy. Weightlessness coated me like chocolate on vanilla ice cream, sweet and ready. When I'd taken vacations in the past, it would take a good two days until the last knot in my gut loosened and I started breathing easily. Then a good two days before returning home, the knots would retie themselves and my gut would tighten again. But this time was different. I was free! No more knots. No more tightness. I wasn't coming back to mountains of messages or to nauseating low-downs on employees or to overdue debts. I wasn't concerned if the exhaust fan broke (or if something evil came out of it!), or if the crack addicts next door ransacked the fourth floor (again). I was sleeping like my favorite puffy, white cloud floating gently in a soft autumn sky.

The Garden of Eden must have been in Hawaii. It was as if my eyes had never seen color before. Black lava, rich green vegetation, deep pink hibiscus. I waded in silk-white sand in an ocean so blue that I kept cupping water in my hands expecting to catch puddles of aqua-tinted liquid. Shells were in incredible variety and abundance. I felt like I was brand new. I even went to a pig roast (every Jewish girl's fantasy) and I swam with dolphins. I relished the tears of overwhelming joy that flowed as I held a thirteen-year-old dolphin named Kona in my arms. This happened the same day Don and I saw dozens of whales perform a water ballet alongside the boat he'd chartered. What a reintroduction to life! I thought I'd never touch down again.

I had been so bogged down with chaos and negatives that I thought my spirituality had deserted me. (More likely, it was I who had deserted my spirituality.) Dr. Ferner assured me that once something is yours, it will always be yours. She also explained, however, that disregarding my soul was one of the reasons for the breakdown in my brain. She said you can't deny what you are made of and if you do, you are likely to become ill. When my spirituality snapped back into me like a thick, stretched rubber band, I found that I hadn't lost any- thing—I'd just forgotten it for a while. And everything seemed clearer and more full of reason than it had before.

Don spent his time on the emerald Hawaiian golf courses and I spent my time by myself on the beaches and loved it. Peacefulness. Tranquility. But it went beyond that. My soul was washed as clean as the debts in my checkbook. There was an unfamiliar energy—not just a flood of contentment, but an unquestionable knowing that from the time I was born, there was meaning in all the choices I had made. Whether good or bad, it was as if all choices were interwoven. There was an intense yearning in me to map it out and actually see the path that was intended for me, to put everything in order and understand that the situations were not given randomly, that each of us is given exclusive opportunities and choices.

While listening to my inner self on the beach, I heard that I should pass on the lessons I've learned and that I should do so with humor, integrity, and candor, and that this is part of my fate. Now I understood the reason to write a book. I felt a grand presence and that I was an integral piece of it, that we are all pieces of it—an infinite connection that will continue forever just as though we were in a club together listening to a band.

You and I may not know each other personally, yet there will come that time when, as the music plays, we clap in rhythm, make eye contact, and smile at one another while enjoying the same thing. We're connected.

I couldn't stay on the beach forever, but I wasn't sad to go home. I was enthusiastic about beginning my new adventures and I was especially excited about writing. It took twelve leg-cramping hours, however, to return to my happy abode from the Aloha State. My muscles felt like a clam that a seagull had smashed against the rocks. Then suddenly as I stood there unlocking our front door, it was as if God blasted me with cool, fresh life. I had just realized I now had only two keys on my Betty Boop key ring! Over the years, I had of necessity accumulated so many keys that my key ring could easily have been considered a lethal weapon: walk-in-refrigerator keys, office keys, second floor keys, third floor door keys, front door keys, file cabinet keys, lockbox keys, wine room keys, bar keys, thermostat-guard keys, cash register keys, freezer keys, liquor room keys, safe keys…keys, keys, and more keys!

I now have a car key and a house key. Another gift of freedom.

FINISHED! FINITO! FINALE!

The lawsuit lasted until May 1999. I'd spent thousands of dollars defending what was mine and it didn't seem fair. But I remembered that I always *knew* there would be a bigger price to pay—much more than the buck it took to buy the original *Carol's* and much more than the money alone. I learned a great deal about myself throughout this entire ordeal. Though I felt I was swindled, I recognized and accepted that all the choices I made were mine. I also knew that I could have gone about things differently. After all, I had allowed Fred to control me just as I'd allowed Deidra to do. I just lacked the self-esteem to believe in and stand up for myself. I have vowed to never again allow myself to feel that inadequate.

The contract Fred finally produced was a copy of a copy of a copy that I still claim never to have signed. It was not dated, there weren't any witnesses, and Fred admitted that he never saw me sign it. I wasted $1,500 hiring two handwriting experts. One of them was willing to testify in court that it wasn't my signature, but the other was unsure. However, there were so many strands woven into this cobweb of a lawsuit that I finally determined that it was better for me to settle and put the whole matter behind me. My attorney said that a jury probably wouldn't believe that anyone could be as ignorant as I had been (he also used the word "stupid"…and I paid him for that) if we went to court.

The lawsuit had demanded an astronomical amount of cash, but when I proved my debts and confirmed that I hadn't a trunk full of currency or any secret bank accounts, we settled on a *much* smaller amount. I smiled when I handed the settlement check to my attorney, for he turned out to be the large man that the tarot card reader saw in my cards more than two years before! I quickly rationalized that if I were to have bought the business outright, I would have paid more than a dollar. It just happened to turn out that I bought *Carol's* after I sold her!

TWO BY SEA

A SLEEPING-DREAM FROM JANUARY 21, 2000

Dad and I were at the seashore. The water was glass clear and I could see some paper littering the floor of the sea. As I held onto the pipe railing beside the four or five concrete stairs that led into the water, a folded newspaper was pushed towards me by a wave. Dad said something about how it doesn't matter how crisp the water looks because there was still some type of pollution interfering with its cleanliness and beauty. It was as if to say that nothing is ever one hundred percent. Nothing is ever truly immaculate.

To the left of the stairs, I could see crabs, lobsters, mussels, and gigantic sea snails clinging to the part of the wall that submerged beneath the water. The lobsters were bright orange in color, the crabs were opaque-white, and the snails dark brown. There were people climbing up the steps from the water. A young, happy father put his smiling five-year-old son on my dad's shoulders to play with him. I was nervous that my father wouldn't be able to withstand the boy's weight and I felt a need to protect my father. Then he swam away from me with the boy still on his shoulders. I thought to myself, *He's not far from me...I can reach him quickly if he goes under*. And he did go under. I swam towards my father as fast as I could and when I got to him, the boy had disappeared and I found my father swimming freely without effort and gliding playfully like a dolphin underneath the crystal water.

PURE PLEASURE

That was the first dream I recall having about my father where I didn't wake up crying, sad, or angry. In that January morning as I recalled the dream, it stunned me when I realized that fact—and *then* my eyes started to well up. It's really working. The forgiveness I've prayed for, the acceptance I've preached to myself and others, and the love that's always been there, now can be felt and is coming full circle. It's not just in the words that come out of my mouth or that I write; it's in the freedom and ease in which my soul is bathing.

I had just come back from Arizona from the "goodbye" visit with Dad. I'd been anxious about it in the days before I left to go see him. *What will I say? How will I feel? How will he feel?* I felt I had already said all that was in me and all that he would allow me to say. But with this visit, it went far beyond.

For the first time ever, my father looked like a dying man, not just a heavy man in a wheelchair. His face was gaunt, his hands thin and trembling, his body distorted and skin discolored, his breathing heavy. My father's body was literally disintegrating from multiple sclerosis, leukemia, and heart disease. He always said, "Only one of 'em will kill me." Few parts of his body worked on him anymore. But wouldn't you know it, I was in the backyard smoking a cigarette when he summoned me into his bedroom. His nose was in perfect working order, for he'd smelled my burning cigarette all the way through brick, siding, and windows. At his bedside, I received the regular sermon about tobacco and then he gave me the ultimate Jewish guilt (and truth): "Here I have a sick body wishing it were healthy, and you have a healthy body, making it sick."

Although he rarely spoke of his parents, a few days before I arrived in Tucson he saw Grandma Esther and Grandfather Mortimer standing at the foot of his bed. He asked Mom if she could see them. She said she didn't. He told her that they smiled at him and kissed him on the cheek. When my mother told me about this, I was happy for him. "They're coming for him, Mom. They will come little by little until he is ready. They're preparing him. That way, he won't be alone." Mom and I were both comforted knowing that. For most of his life, my father had chosen solitude over his family.

To say we made "peace" with one another sounds like we were at war, but I don't know how else to put it. Dad was proud of me and he was thrilled about the fact that I was writing this book. Although I'm sure he knew he would never see the book in its final form, he said he believed I'd have a bestseller on my hands. His main concern was that the publisher-to-be would have sufficient means with which to keep up with the purchasing demands!

Every day that I was there, I sat on his bed and read him stories. And not just the funny ones, but also personal ones that dealt with him and with the problems we'd had. My father was so unbiased. Even the parts I knew must have stung him he validated by saying, "It's your story. You have every right to write your life the way you lived it." He closed his eyes and listened with his mind, painting each sentence into a picture. I watched him do this. If a word didn't make sense or seemed like the wrong word to use, he'd put up his hand to stop me. He'd ask me what I was trying to say and then give me suggestions. It's funny, in the past when he would correct me or offer suggestions, I would feel my blood pressure rise and the tips of my ears would get hot. But that didn't happen. This time, we were both doing much more than hearing with our ears.

Although my plane back to Cincinnati left very early on a Sunday morning, Dad made it a point to wake up to see me off. We both knew that this would very likely be the last time that we would see each other. He told me he wished I lived closer so he could see me again. I said I wished I did, too.

My emotions were naked and full. I wanted to curl into him like I did as a child early on the weekend mornings when I'd barge into my parents' bedroom. But for some reason, I didn't want to disturb the past. I knew that I wanted to keep what I had, that it should be adored and held as is, that I wouldn't be able to recreate my Saturday morning little girl sleepy-play with him. So instead, I sat in his wheelchair that was parked beside his bed and looked at my crippled father and kissed him several times on the cheek. Dad kissed me back and we confirmed our love for one another. Our future had never felt so cloudless.

It was such a good visit and the night I returned home, I called my parents. Mom also felt high from my visit and said that Dad told her that I was *pure pleasure*. He's never said that about me before. I asked to talk to Dad. When he got on the phone, I told him how much I enjoyed the time we spent together. "I'm glad we aired some things," he said to me.

"It's too bad that we don't have more time to collaborate our talents for my book, Dad. But I can't tell you how happy I am that we captured the chance to allow it to happen now."

"Me, too, Carol, me, too. Maybe in the future…"

"Maybe so dad…maybe so."

Michael Alonzo Sherman
June 6, 1932 – January 24, 2000

THE GAMUT – #2

I was just as comfortable at my engagement party thrown by Forbes magazine millionaires who lived in a home built by Frank Lloyd Wright as I was at my bachelorette party held in my honor at a gay leather bar. I know how frustrating it feels to be in discord with my body while trying a multitude of anti-depressants that are aimed to help me and know the relief felt when a particular combination finally works. I know how it feels when a business mangles a friendship and how it feels to unite that friendship I thought lost. I know how it feels to wrestle a midget in lime Jell-O and…well…jeez…I *still* can't find anything to compare with that!

I know how it feels to be controlled by someone and know how it feels to command my own life. I know the pride of having a business succeed and the desperation of having a business fail. I know the hypocrisy of wanting to live a long and happy life but continuing to smoke cigarettes. I know how it feels to think I couldn't make it on my own and how exhilarating it is to find out I could. I know how hopeless it feels to lose countless friends to AIDS. I also know the hope felt when medical treatments succeed in making the presence of AIDS less detectable in friends.

I know the difference between being the clown everyone laughs at and the entertainer everyone laughs with. I know how it feels to forgive people who have hurt me badly and I know how unjust I feel towards myself when I don't. I know how it feels to have the world crash around me and also how it feels to think I was holding the world with just one finger. I know how to dream.

I want to keep adding to my list.

Other Fine Titles From
Five Star Publications, Incorporated

Most titles are available through
www.BarnesandNoble.com and www.amazon.com

Shakespeare: To Teach or Not to Teach
By Cass Foster and Lynn G. Johnson
The answer is a resounding "To Teach!" There's nothing dull about this guide for anyone teaching Shakespeare in the classroom, with activities such as crossword puzzles, a scavenger hunt, warm-up games, and costume and scenery suggestions.
ISBN 1-877749-03-6

The Sixty-Minute Shakespeare Series
By Cass Foster
Not enough time to tackle the unabridged versions of the world's most widely read playwright? Pick up a copy of *Romeo and Juliet* (ISBN 1-877749-38-9), *A Midsummer Night's Dream* (ISBN 1-877749-37-0), *Hamlet* (ISBN 1-877749-40-0), *Macbeth* (ISBN 1-877749-41-9), *Much Ado About Nothing* (ISBN 1-877749-42-7), and *Twelfth Night* (ISBN 1-877749-39-7) and discover how much more accessible Shakespeare can be to you and your students.

Shakespeare for Children: The Story of Romeo and Juliet
By Cass Foster
Adults shouldn't keep a classic this good to themselves. This fully illustrated book makes the play easily understandable to young readers, yet it is faithful to the spirit of the original. A *Benjamin Franklin Children's Storybooks Award* nominee.
ISBN 0-9619853-3-x

The Adventures of Andi O'Malley
By Celeste Messer

(1) Angel Experiment JR134
Ashley Layne is the richest and most popular girl in school. In an unusual twist, Andi is given the opportunity to know what it's truly like to be Ashley Layne. Travel with Andi as she discovers that things are not always as they seem.   ISBN 0-9702171-0-2

(2) The Broken Wing
Andi is visited by a little angel who needs her help in more ways than one. The angel has broken her wing in a midair collision with another, larger angel and desperately needs Andi to hide her while she heals. Rather than hide her, Andi takes the little angel to school with her where no one could have expected the lessons they would learn!
ISBN 0-9702171-1-0

(3) The Gift
Andi receives an assignment from her guardian angel. At first, she's excited, but she becomes furious when she realizes what the job involves. Although Andi tries desperately to get out of completing her assignment, she learns there is no turning back. What happens in the end could only happen to Andi O'Malley!
ISBN 0-9702171-3-7

Other Fine Titles From
Five Star Publications, Incorporated

Most titles are available through
www.BarnesandNoble.com and www.amazon.com

(4) Circle of Light

The world is about to be taken over by Zykien, the most evil of all angels of darkness. With the help of the rather odd-looking Miss Bluebonnet, Andi and her friends discover the incredible power of goodness that can result when people work together. Even the Tashonians, the tiniest of creatures, play an important role in restoring peace and love to the world. ISBN 0-9702171-2-9

(5) Three Miracles

Three young people are in a terrible accident caused by a drunk driver. Their voices are heard—but only by Andi's friend Troy. When he proves to Andi and her sister and brother that he's not making it up, the three voices give them three tasks that will change their lives and the lives of several others forever. ISBN 0-9702171-4-5

Letters of Love: Stories from the Heart

Edited by Salvatore Caputo
In this warm collection of love letters and stories, a group of everyday people share hopes, dreams, and experiences of love: love won, love lost, and love found again. Most of all, they share their belief that love is a blessing that makes life's challenges worthwhile. ISBN 1-877749-35-4

Linda F. Radke's Promote Like a Pro: Small Budget, Big Show

By Linda F. Radke
In this step-by-step guide, self-publishers can learn how to use the print and broadcast media, public relations, the Internet, public speaking, and other tools to market books—without breaking the bank! In *Linda F. Radke's Promote Like a Pro: Small Budget, Big Show*, a successful publisher and a group of insiders offer self-publishers valuable information about promoting books. ISBN 1-877749-36-2

The Economical Guide to Self-Publishing: How to Produce and Market Your Book on a Budget

By Linda F. Radke
This book is a must-have for anyone who is or wants to be a self-publisher. It is a valuable step-by-step guide for producing and promoting your book effectively, even on a limited budget. The book is filled with tips on avoiding common, costly mistakes and provides resources that can save you lots of money—not to mention headaches. A *Writer's Digest Book Club* selection. ISBN 1-877749-16-8

That Hungarian's in My Kitchen

By Linda F. Radke
You won't want that Hungarian to leave your kitchen after you've tried some of the 125 Hungarian-American Kosher recipes that fill this delightful cookbook. Written for both the novice cook and the sophisticated chef, the cookbook comes complete with "Aunt Ethel's Helpful Hints." ISBN 1-877749-28-1

Other Fine Titles From
Five Star Publications, Incorporated

Most titles are available through
www.BarnesandNoble.com and www.amazon.com

Kosher Kettle: International Adventures in Jewish Cooking

By Sybil Ruth Kaplan, Foreword by Joan Nathan

With more than 350 recipes from 27 countries, this is one Kosher cookbook you don't want to be without. It includes everything from wheat halva from India to borrekas from Greece. Five Star Publications is donating a portion of all sales of *Kosher Kettle* to MAZON: A Jewish Response to Hunger. A *Jewish Book Club* selection. ISBN 1-877749-19-2

Passover Cookery

By Joan Kekst

Whether you're a novice or an experienced cook, Passover can result in hours spent hunting down recipes from friends and family or scrambling through piles of cookbooks. Now Passover cooking can become "a piece of cake" with the new book, *Passover Cookery: In the Kitchen with Joan Kekst*. You can create a new, distinctive feast or reproduce the beautiful traditions from your grandmother's Seder with Kekst's easy to follow steps and innovative recipes from her extensive private collection. From daily fare to gourmet, "kosher for Passover" delights have never been easier or more delicious! ISBN 1-877749-44-3

Household Careers: Nannies, Butlers, Maids & More: The Complete Guide for Finding Household Employment

By Linda F. Radke

Numerous professional positions are available in the child-care and home-help fields. This award-winning book provides all the information you need to find and secure a household job. ISBN 1-877749-05-2

Nannies, Maids & More: The Complete Guide for Hiring Household Help

By Linda F. Radke

Anyone who has had to hire household help knows what a challenge it can be. This book provides a step-by-step guide to hiring—and keeping—household help, complete with sample ads, interview questions, and employment forms. ISBN 0-9619853-2-1

Shoah: Journey From the Ashes

By Cantor Leo Fettman and Paul M. Howey

Cantor Leo Fettman survived the horrors of Auschwitz while millions of others, including almost his entire family, did not. He worked in the crematorium, was a victim of Dr. Josef Mengele's experiments, and lived through an attempted hanging by the SS. His remarkable tale of survival and subsequent joy is an inspiration for all. *Shoah* includes a historical prologue that chronicles the 2,000 years of anti-Semitism that led to the Holocaust. Cantor Fettman's message is one of love and hope, yet it contains an important warning for new generations to remember so the evils of the past will not be repeated. ISBN 0-9679721-0-8

Other Fine Titles From
Five Star Publications, Incorporated

Most titles are available through
www.BarnesandNoble.com and www.amazon.com

The Proper Pig's Guide to Mealtime Manners
By L.A. Kowal and Sally Starbuck Stamp
No one in your family would ever act like a pig at mealtime, but perhaps you know another family with that problem. This whimsical guide, complete with its own ceramic pig, gives valuable advice for children and adults alike on how to make mealtimes more fun and mannerly.
ISBN 1-877749-20-6

Junk Mail Solution
By Jackie Plusch
Jackie Plusch's Junk Mail Solution can help stop the aggravating intrusion of unwanted solicitations by both mail and phone. She offers three easy steps for freeing yourself from junk mailers and telemarketers. The book also includes pre-addressed cards to major mass marketing companies and handy script cards to put by your phones.   ISBN 0-9673136-1-9